THE TEMPLE *and* A PRIEST *to the* TEMPLE

By

George Herbert

Edited by

A. R. Waller

19 02

LONDON: J. M. DENT & CO.
29 & 30, *Bedford Street, Covent Garden*
W.C.

THE TEMPLE.

SACRED POEMS AND PRIVATE EJA-CULATIONS.

By Mr. GEORGE HERBERT.

PSAL. 29.

In his Temple doth every man ſpeak of his honour.

CAMBRIDGE:
Printed by *Thom. Buck*,
and *Roger Daniel*, printers
to the Univerſitie.
1633.

The Dedication.

Lord, my first fruits present themselves to thee ;
Yet not mine neither : for from thee they came,
And must return. Accept of them and me,
And make us strive, who shall sing best thy name.
Turn their eyes hither, who shall make a gain :
Theirs, who shall hurt themselves or me, refrain.

THE PRINTERS TO THE READER

THE dedication of this work having been made by the Authour to the *Divine Majestie* onely, how should we now presume to interest any mortall man in the patronage of it? Much lesse think we it meet to seek the recommendation of the Muses, for that which himself was confident to have been inspired by a diviner breath then flows from *Helicon*. The world therefore shall receive it in that naked simplicitie, with which he left it, without any addition either of support or ornament, more then is included in it self. We leave it free and unforestalled to every mans judgement, and to the benefit that he shall finde by perusall. Onely for the clearing of some passages, we have thought it not unfit to make the common Reader privie to some few particularities of the condition and disposition of the Person;

Being nobly born, and as eminently endued with gifts of the minde, and having by industrie and happy education perfected them to that great height of excellencie, whereof his fellowship of Trinitie Colledge in Cambridge, and his Orator-ship in the Universitie, together with that knowledge which the Kings Court had taken of him, could make relation farre above ordinarie. Quitting both his deserts and all the opportunities that he had for worldly preferment, he betook himself to the Sanctuarie and Temple of God, choosing rather to serve at Gods Altar, then to seek the honour of State-employments. As for those inward enforcements to this course (for outward there was none) which many of these ensuing verses bear witnesse of, they detract not from the freedome, but adde to the honour of this resolution in him. As God had enabled him, so he accounted him meet not onely to be called, but to be compelled to this service: Wherein his faithfull discharge was such, as may make him justly a companion to the primitive Saints, and a pattern or more for the age he lived in.

To testifie his independencie upon all others, and to quicken his diligence in this kinde, he used in his ordinarie speech, when he made mention of the blessed name of our Lord and Saviour Jesus Christ, to adde, *My Master.*

Next God, he loved that which God himself hath magnified above all things, that is, his Word: so as he hath been heard to make solemne protestation, that he would not part with one leaf thereof for the whole world, if it were offered him in exchange.

His obedience and conformitie to the Church and the discipline thereof was singularly remarkable. Though he abounded in private devotions, yet went he every morning and evening with his familie to the Church; and by his example, exhortations, and encouragements drew the greater part of his parishioners to accompanie him dayly in the publick celebration of Divine Service.

As for worldly matters, his love and esteem to them was so little, as no man can more ambitiously seek, then he did earnestly endeavour the resignation of an Ecclesiasticall dignitie, which he was possessour of. But God permitted not the accomplishment of this desire, having ordained him his instrument for reedifying of the Church belonging thereunto, that had layen ruinated almost twenty yeares. The reparation whereof, having been uneffectually attempted by publick collections, was in the end by his own and some few others private free-will-offerings succesfully effected. With the remembrance whereof, as of an especiall good work, when a friend went about to comfort him on his death-bed, he made answer, *It is a good work, if it be sprinkled with the bloud of Christ:* otherwise then in this respect he could finde nothing to glorie or comfort himself with, neither in this, nor in any other thing.

And these are but a few of many that might be said, which we have chosen to premise as a glance to some parts of the ensuing book, and for an example to the Reader. We conclude all with his own Motto, with which he used to conclude all things that might seem to tend any way to his own honour;

Lesse then the least of Gods mercies.

The Temple

THE CHURCH-PORCH

Perirrhanterium

THOU, whose sweet youth and early hopes inhance
Thy rate and price, and mark thee for a treasure;
Hearken unto a Verser, who may chance
Ryme thee to good, and make a bait of pleasure.
A verse may finde him, who a sermon flies,
And turn delight into a sacrifice.

Beware of lust: it doth pollute and foul
Whom God in Baptisme washt with his own blood.
It blots thy lesson written in thy soul;
The holy lines cannot be understood.
How dare those eyes upon a Bible look,
Much lesse towards God, whose lust is all their book?

Abstain wholly, or wed. Thy bounteous Lord
Allows thee choise of paths: take no by-wayes;
But gladly welcome what he doth afford;
Not grudging, that thy lust hath bounds and staies.
Continence hath his joy: weigh both; and so
If rottennesse have more, let Heaven go.

If God had laid all common, certainly
Man would have been th'incloser: but since now
God hath impal'd us on the contrarie
Man breaks the fence, and every ground will plough.
  O what were man, might he himself misplace
  Sure to be crosse he would shift feet and face.

Drink not the third glasse, which thou canst not tame,
When once it is within thee; but before
Mayst rule it, as thou list; and poure the shame,
Which it would poure on thee, upon the floore.
  It is most just to throw that on the ground,
  Which would throw me there, if I keep the round.

He that is drunken, may his mother kill
Bigge with his sister: he hath lost the reins,
Is outlaw'd by himself: all kinde of ill
Did with his liquour slide into his veins.
  The drunkard forfets Man, and doth devest
  All worldly right, save what he hath by beast.

Shall I, to please anothers wine-sprung minde,
Lose all mine own? God hath giv'n me a measure
Short of his canne, and bodie; must I finde
A pain in that, wherein he findes a pleasure?
  Stay at the third glasse: if thou lose thy hold,
  Then thou are modest, and the wine grows bold.

If reason move not Gallants, quit the room,
(All in a shipwrack shift their severall way)
Let not a common ruine thee intombe:
Be not a beast in courtesie; but stay,
  Stay at the third cup, or forgo the place.
  Wine above all things doth Gods stamp deface.

Yet, if thou sinne in wine or wantonnesse,
Boast not thereof; nor make thy shame thy glorie.
Frailtie gets pardon by submissivenesse;
But he that boasts, shuts that out of his storie.
He makes flat warre with God, and doth defie
With his poore clod of earth the spacious sky.

Take not his name, who made thy mouth, in vain:
It gets thee nothing, and hath no excuse.
Lust and wine plead a pleasure, avarice gain:
But the cheap swearer through his open sluce
Lets his soul runne for nought, as little fearing.
Were I an *Epicure*, I could bate swearing.

When thou dost tell anothers jest, therein
Omit the oathes, which true wit cannot need:
Pick out of tales the mirth, but not the sinne.
He pares his apple, that will cleanly feed.
Play not away the vertue of that name,
Which is thy best stake, when griefs make thee tame.

The cheapest sinnes most dearely punisht are;
Because to shun them also is so cheap:
For we have wit to mark them, and to spare.
O crumble not away thy souls fair heap.
If thou wilt die, the gates of hell are broad:
Pride and full sinnes have made the way a road.

Lie not; but let thy heart be true to God,
Thy mouth to it, thy actions to them both:
Cowards tell lies, and those that fear the rod;
The stormie working soul spits lies and froth.
Dare to be true. Nothing can need a ly:
A fault, which needs it most, grows two thereby.

Flie idlenesse, which yet thou canst not flie
By dressing, mistressing, and complement.
If those take up thy day, the sunne will crie
Against thee: for his light was onely lent.
  God gave thy soul brave wings; put not those feathers
  Into a bed, to sleep out all ill weathers.

Art thou a Magistrate? then be severe:
If studious; copie fair, what time hath blurr'd;
Redeem truth from his jawes: if souldier,
Chase brave employments with a naked sword
  Throughout the world. Fool not: for all may have,
  If they dare try, a glorious life, or grave.

O England! full of sinne, but most of sloth;
Spit out thy flegme, and fill thy brest with glorie:
Thy Gentrie bleats, as if thy native cloth
Transfus'd a sheepishnesse into thy storie:
  Not that they all are so; but that the most
  Are gone to grasse, and in the pasture lost.

This losse springs chiefly from our education.
Some till their ground, but let weeds choke their sonne:
Some mark a partridge, never their childes fashion:
Some ship them over, and the thing is done.
  Studie this art, make it thy great designe;
  And if Gods image move thee not, let thine.

Some great estates provide, but doe not breed
A mast'ring minde; so both are lost thereby:
Or els they breed them tender, make them need
All that they leave: this is flat povertie.
  For he, that needs five thousand pound to live,
  Is full as poore as he, that needs but five.

The way to make thy sonne rich, is to fill
His minde with rest, before his trunk with riches:
For wealth without contentment, climbes a hill
To feel those tempests, which fly over ditches.
  But if thy sonne can make ten pound his measure,
  Then all thou addest may be call'd his treasure.

When thou dost purpose ought, (within thy power)
Be sure to doe it, though it be but small:
Constancie knits the bones, and makes us stowre,
When wanton pleasures becken us to thrall.
  Who breaks his own bond, forfeiteth himself:
  What nature made a ship, he makes a shelf.

Doe all things like a man, not sneakingly:
Think the king sees thee still; for his King does.
Simpring is but a lay-hypocrisie:
Give it a corner, and the clue undoes.
  Who fears to do ill, sets himself to task:
  Who fears to do well, sure should wear a mask.

Look to thy mouth; diseases enter there.
Thou hast two sconses, if thy stomack call;
Carve, or discourse; do not a famine fear.
Who carves, is kind to two; who talks, to all.
  Look on meat, think it dirt, then eat a bit;
  And say withall, Earth to earth I commit.

Slight those who say amidst their sickly healths,
Thou liv'st by rule. What doth not so, but man?
Houses are built by rule, and common-wealths.
Entice the trusty sunne, if that you can,
  From his Ecliptick line: becken the skie.
  Who lives by rule then, keeps good companie.

Who keeps no guard upon himself, is slack,
And rots to nothing at the next great thaw.
Man is a shop of rules, a well truss'd pack,
Whose every parcell under-writes a law.
  Lose not thy self, nor give thy humours way:
  God gave them to thee under lock and key.

By all means use sometimes to be alone.
Salute thy self: see what thy soul doth wear.
Dare to look in thy chest; for 'tis thine own:
And tumble up and down what thou find'st there.
  Who cannot rest till hee good fellows finde,
  He breaks up house, turns out of doores his minde.

Be thriftie, but not covetous: therefore give
Thy need, thine honour, and thy friend his due.
Never was scraper brave man. Get to live;
Then live, and use it: els, it is not true
  That thou hast gotten. Surely use alone
  Makes money not a contemptible stone.

Never exceed thy income. Youth may make
Ev'n with the yeare: but age, if it will hit,
Shoots a bow short, and lessens still his stake,
As the day lessens, and his life with it.
  Thy children, kindred, friends upon thee call;
  Before thy journey fairly part with all.

Yet in thy thriving still misdoubt some evil;
Lest gaining gain on thee, and make thee dimme
To all things els. Wealth is the conjurers devil;
Whom when he thinks he hath, the devil hath him.
  Gold thou mayst safely touch; but if it stick
  Unto thy hands, it woundeth to the quick.

What skills it, if a bag of stones or gold
About thy neck do drown thee? raise thy head;
Take starres for money; starres not to be told
By any art, yet to be purchased.
  None is so wastefull as the scraping dame.
  She loseth three for one; her soul, rest, fame.

By no means runne in debt: take thine own measure.
Who cannot live on twentie pound a yeare,
Cannot on fourtie: he's a man of pleasure,
A kinde of thing that's for it self too deere.
  The curious unthrift makes his cloth too wide,
  And spares himself, but would his taylor chide.

Spend not on hopes. They that by pleading clothes
Do fortunes seek, when worth and service fail,
Would have their tale beleeved for their oathes,
And are like empty vessels under sail.
  Old courtiers know this; therefore set out so,
  As all the day thou mayst hold out to go.

In clothes, cheap handsomnesse doth bear the bell.
Wisedome's a trimmer thing, then shop e're gave.
Say not then, This with that lace will do well;
But, This with my discretion will be brave.
  Much curiousnesse is a perpetuall wooing
  Nothing with labour; folly long a doing.

Play not for gain, but sport. Who playes for more,
Then he can lose with pleasure, stakes his heart;
Perhaps his wives too, and whom she hath bore:
Servants and churches also play their part.
  Onely a herauld, who that way doth passe,
  Findes his crackt name at length in the church-glasse.

If yet thou love game at so deere a rate,
Learn this, that hath old gamesters deerely cost:
Dost lose? rise up: dost winne? rise in that state.
Who strive to sit out losing hands, are lost.
  Game is a civil gunpowder, in peace
  Blowing up houses with their whole increase.

In conversation boldnesse now bears sway.
But know, that nothing can so foolish be,
As empty boldnesse: therefore first assay
To stuffe thy minde with solid braverie;
  Then march on gallant: get substantiall worth.
  Boldnesse guilds finely, and will set it forth.

Be sweet to all. Is thy complexion sowre?
Then keep such companie; make them thy allay:
Get a sharp wife, a servant that will lowre.
A stumbler stumbles least in rugged way.
  Command thy self in chief. He lifes warre knows,
  Whom all his passions follow, as he goes.

Catch not at quarrels. He that dares not speak
Plainly and home, is coward of the two.
Think not thy fame at ev'ry twitch will break:
By great deeds shew, that thou canst little do;
  And do them not: that shall thy wisdome be.;
  And change thy temperance into braverie.

If that thy fame with ev'ry toy be pos'd,
'Tis a thinne webbe, which poysonous fancies make:
But the great souldiers honour was compos'd
Of thicker stuffe, which would endure a shake.
  Wisdome picks friends; civilitie playes the rest.
  A toy shunn'd cleanly passeth with the best.

Laugh not too much: the wittie man laughs least:
For wit is newes onely to ignorance.
Lesse at thine own things laugh; lest in the jest
Thy person share, and the conceit advance.
  Make not thy sport, abuses: for the fly
  That feeds on dung, is coloured thereby.

Pick out of mirth, like stones out of thy ground,
Profanenesse, filthinesse, abusivenesse.
These are the scumme, with which course wits abound:
The fine may spare these well, yet not go lesse.
  All things are bigge with jest: nothing that's plain,
  But may be wittie, if thou hast the vein.

Wit's an unruly engine, wildly striking
Sometimes a friend, sometimes the engineer.
Hast thou the knack? pamper it not with liking:
But if thou want it, buy it not too deere.
  Many affecting wit beyond their power,
  Have got to be a deare fool for an houre.

A sad wise valour is the brave complexion,
That leads the van, and swallows up the cities.
The gigler is a milk-maid, whom infection,
Or a fir'd beacon frighteth from his ditties.
  Then he's the sport: the mirth then in him rests,
  And the sad man is cock of all his jests.

Towards great persons use respective boldnesse:
That temper gives them theirs, and yet doth take
Nothing from thine: in service, care, or coldnesse
Doth ratably thy fortunes marre or make.
  Feed no man in his sinnes: for adulation
  Doth make thee parcell-devil in damnation.

Envie not greatnesse : for thou mak'st thereby
Thy self the worse, and so the distance greater.
Be not thine own worm : yet such jealousie,
As hurts not others, but may make thee better,
  Is a good spurre. Correct thy passions spite ;
  Then may the beasts draw thee to happy light.

When basenesse is exalted, do not bate
The place its honour, for the persons sake.
The shrine is that which thou dost venerate ;
And not the beast, that bears it on his back.
  I care not though the cloth of state should be
  Not of rich arras, but mean tapestrie.

Thy friend put in thy bosome : wear his eies
Still in thy heart, that he may see what's there.
If cause require, thou art his sacrifice ;
Thy drops of bloud must pay down all his fear :
  But love is lost ; the way of friendship's gone,
  Though *David* had his *Jonathan*, *Christ* his *John*.

Yet be not surety, if thou be a father.
Love is a personall debt. I cannot give
My childrens right, nor ought he take it : rather
Both friends should die, then hinder them to live.
  Fathers first enter bonds to natures ends ;
  And are her sureties, ere they are a friends.

If thou be single, all thy goods and ground
Submit to love ; but yet not more then all.
Give one estate, as one life. None is bound
To work for two, who brought himself to thrall.
  God made me one man ; love makes me no more,
  Till labour come, and make my weaknesse score.

In thy discourse, if thou desire to please:
All such is courteous, usefull, new, or wittie.
Usefulnesse comes by labour, wit by ease;
Courtesie grows in court; news in the citie.
  Get a good stock of these, then draw the card;
  That suites him best, of whom thy speech is heard.

Entice all neatly to what they know best;
For so thou dost thy self and him a pleasure:
(But a proud ignorance will lose his rest,
Rather then shew his cards) steal from his treasure
  What to ask further. Doubts well rais'd do lock
  The speaker to thee, and preserve thy stock.

If thou be Master-gunner, spend not all
That thou canst speak, at once; but husband it,
And give men turns of speech: do not forestall
By lavishnesse thine own, and others wit,
  As if thou mad'st thy will. A civil guest
  Will no more talk all, then eat all the feast.

Be calm in arguing: for fiercenesse makes
Errour a fault, and truth discourtesie.
Why should I feel another mans mistakes
More, then his sicknesses or povertie?
  In love I should: but anger is not love,
  Nor wisdome neither: therefore gently move.

Calmnesse is great advantage: he that lets
Another chafe, may warm him at his fire:
Mark all his wandrings, and enjoy his frets;
As cunning fencers suffer heat to tire.
  Truth dwels not in the clouds: the bow that's there,
  Doth often aim at, never hit the sphere.

Mark what another sayes : for many are
Full of themselves, and answer their own notion.
Take all into thee ; then with equall care
Ballance each dramme of reason, like a potion.
  If truth be with thy friend, be with them both :
  Share in the conquest, and confesse a troth.

Be usefull where thou livest, that they may
Both want, and wish thy pleasing presence still.
Kindnesse, good parts, great places are the way
To compasse this. Finde out mens wants and will,
  And meet them there. All worldly joyes go lesse
  To the one joy of doing kindnesses.

Pitch thy behaviour low, thy projects high ;
So shalt thou humble and magnanimous be :
Sink not in spirit : who aimeth at the sky,
Shoots higher much then he that means a tree.
  A grain of glorie mixt with humblenesse
  Cures both a fever and lethargicknesse.

Let thy minde still be bent, still plotting where,
And when, and how the businesse may be done.
Slacknesse breeds worms ; but the sure traveller,
Though he alight sometimes, still goeth on.
  Active and stirring spirits live alone.
  Write on the others, Here lies such a one.

Slight not the smallest losse, whether it be
In love or honour : take account of all ;
Shine like the sunne in every corner : see
Whether thy stock of credit swell, or fall.
  Who say, I care not, those I give for lost ;
  And to instruct them, 'twill not quit the cost.

Scorn no mans love, though of a mean degree;
(Love is a present for a mightie king)
Much lesse make any one thine enemie.
As gunnes destroy, so may a little sling.
 The cunning workman never doth refuse
 The meanest tool, that he may chance to use.

All forrain wisdome doth amount to this,
To take all that is given; whether wealth,
Or love, or language; nothing comes amisse:
A good digestion turneth all to health:
 And then as farre as fair behaviour may,
 Strike off all scores; none are so cleare as they.

Keep all thy native good, and naturalize
All forrain of that name; but scorn their ill:
Embrace their activenesse, not vanities.
Who follows all things, forfeiteth his will.
 If thou observest strangers in each fit,
 In time they'l runne thee out of all thy wit.

Affect in things about thee cleanlinesse,
That all may gladly board thee, as a flowre.
Slovens take up their stock of noisomnesse
Beforehand, and anticipate their last houre.
 Let thy mindes sweetnesse have his operation
 Upon thy body, clothes, and habitation.

In Almes regard thy means, and others merit.
Think heav'n a better bargain, then to give
Onely thy single market-money for it.
Joyn hands with God to make a man to live.
 Give to all something; to a good poore man,
 Till thou change names, and be where he began.

Man is Gods image; but a poore man is
Christs stamp to boot: both images regard.
God reckons for him, counts the favour his:
Write, So much giv'n to God; thou shalt be heard.
  Let thy almes go before, and keep heav'ns gate
  Open for thee; or both may come too late.

Restore to God his due in tithe and time:
A tithe purloin'd cankers the whole estate.
Sundaies observe: think when the bells do chime,
'Tis angels musick; therefore come not late.
  God then deals blessings: If a king did so,
  Who would not haste, nay give, to see the show?

Twice on the day his due is understood;
For all the week thy food so oft he gave thee.
Thy cheere is mended; bate not of the food,
Because 'tis better, and perhaps may save thee.
  Thwart not th' Almighty God: O be not crosse.
  Fast when thou wilt; but then 'tis gain, not losse.

Though private prayer be a brave designe,
Yet publick hath more promises, more love:
And love's a weight to hearts, to eies a signe.
We all are but cold suitours; let us move
  Where it is warmest. Leave thy six and seven;
  Pray with the most: for where most pray, is heaven.

When once thy foot enters the church, be bare.
God is more there, then thou: for thou art there
Onely by his permission. Then beware,
And make thy self all reverence and fear.
  Kneeling ne're spoil'd silk stocking: quit thy state.
  All equall are within the churches gate.

Resort to sermons, but to prayers most:
Praying 's the end of preaching. O be drest;
Stay not for th' other pin: why thou hast lost
A joy for it worth worlds. Thus hell doth jest
  Away thy blessings, and extreamly flout thee,
  Thy clothes being fast, but thy soul loose about thee.

In time of service seal up both thine eies,
And send them to thine heart; that spying sinne,
They may weep out the stains by them did rise:
Those doores being shut, all by the eare comes in.
  Who marks in church-time others symmetrie,
  Makes all their beautie his deformitie.

Let vain or busie thoughts have there no part:
Bring not thy plough, thy plots, thy pleasures thither.
Christ purg'd his temple; so must thou thy heart.
All worldly thoughts are but theeves met together
  To couzin thee. Look to thy actions well:
  For churches are either our heav'n or hell.

Judge not the preacher; for he is thy Judge:
If thou mislike him, thou conceiv'st him not.
God calleth preaching folly. Do not grudge
To pick out treasures from an earthen pot.
  The worst speak something good: if all want sense,
  God takes a text, and preacheth patience.

He that gets patience, and the blessing which
Preachers conclude with, hath not lost his pains.
He that by being at church escapes the ditch,
Which he might fall in by companions, gains.
  He that loves Gods abode, and to combine
  With saints on earth, shall one day with them shine.

Jest not at preachers language, or expression:
How know'st thou, but thy sinnes made him miscarrie?
Then turn thy faults and his into confession:
God sent him, whatsoe're he be: O tarry,
  And love him for his Master: his condition,
  Though it be ill, makes him no ill Physician.

None shall in hell such bitter pangs endure,
As those, who mock at Gods way of salvation.
Whom oil and balsames kill, what salve can cure?
They drink with greedinesse a full damnation.
  The Jews refused thunder; and we, folly.
  Though God do hedge us in, yet who is holy?

Summe up at night, what thou hast done by day;
And in the morning, what thou hast to do.
Dresse and undresse thy soul: mark the decay
And growth of it: if with thy watch, that too
  Be down, then winde up both, since we shall be
  Most surely judg'd, make thy accounts agree.

In brief, acquit thee bravely; play the man.
Look not on pleasures as they come, but go.
Deferre not the least vertue: lifes poore span
Make not an ell, by trifling in thy wo.
  If thou do ill; the joy fades, not the pains:
  If well; the pain doth fade, the joy remains.

SUPERLIMINARE

Thou, whom the former precepts have
Sprinkled and taught, how to behave
Thy self in church; approach, and taste
The churches mysticall repast.

Avoid profanenesse; come not here:
Nothing but holy, pure, and cleare,
Or that which groneth to be so,
May at his perill further go.

THE ALTAR

A broken ALTAR, Lord, thy servant reares,
Made of a heart, and cemented with teares:
Whose parts are as thy hand did frame;
No workmans tool hath touch'd the same.
A HEART alone
Is such a stone,
As nothing but
Thy pow'r doth cut.
Wherefore each part
Of my hard heart
Meets in this frame,
To praise thy name.
That if I chance to hold my peace,
These stones to praise thee may not cease.
O let thy blessed SACRIFICE be mine,
And sanctifie this ALTAR to be thine.

THE SACRIFICE

THE SACRIFICE

Oh all ye, who passe by, whose eyes and minde
To worldly things are sharp, but to me blinde;
To me, who took eyes that I might you finde:
Was ever grief like mine?

The Princes of my people make a head
Against their Maker: they do wish me dead,
Who cannot wish, except I give them bread:
Was ever grief like mine?

Without me each one, who doth now me brave,
Had to this day been an Egyptian slave.
They use that power against me, which I gave:
Was ever grief like mine?

Mine own Apostle, who the bag did beare,
Though he had all I had, did not forbeare
To sell me also, and to put me there:
Was ever grief, &c.

For thirtie pence he did my death devise,
Who at three hundred did the ointment prize,
Not half so sweet as my sweet sacrifice:
Was ever grief, &c.

Therefore my soul melts, and my hearts deare treasure
Drops bloud (the onely beads) my words to measure:
O let this cup passe, if it be thy pleasure:
Was ever grief, &c.

These drops being temper'd with a sinners tears,
A Balsome are for both the Hemispheres:
Curing all wounds, but mine; all, but my fears:
Was ever grief like mine?

Yet my Disciples sleep: I cannot gain
One houre of watching; but their drowsie brain
Comforts not me, and doth my doctrine stain:
Was ever grief, &c.

Arise, arise, they come. Look how they runne.
Alas! what haste they make to be undone!
How with their lanterns do they seek the sunne!
Was ever grief, &c.

With clubs and staves they seek me, as a thief,
Who am the way of truth, the true relief;
Most true to those, who are my greatest grief:
Was ever grief, &c.

Judas, dost thou betray me with a kisse?
Canst thou finde hell about my lips? and misse
Of life, just at the gates of life and blisse?
Was ever grief, &c.

See, they lay hold on me, not with the hands
Of faith, but furie: yet at their commands
I suffer binding, who have loos'd their bands:
Was ever grief, &c.

All my Disciples flie; fear puts a barre
Betwixt my friends and me. They leave the starre,
That brought the wise men of the East from farre.
Was ever grief, &c.

Then from one ruler to another bound
They leade me; urging, that it was not sound
What I taught: Comments would the text confound.
Was ever grief like mine?

The Priest and rulers all false witnesse seek
'Gainst him, who seeks not life, but is the meek
And readie Paschal Lambe of this great week:
Was ever grief, &c.

Then they accuse me of great blasphemie,
That I did thrust into the Deitie,
Who never thought that any robberie:
Was ever grief, &c.

Some said, that I the Temple to the floore
In three dayes raz'd, and raised as before.
Why, he that built the world can do much more:
Was ever grief, &c.

Then they condemne me all with that same breath,
Which I do give them daily, unto death.
Thus *Adam* my first breathing rendereth:
Was ever grief, &c.

They binde, and leade me unto *Herod:* he
Sends me to *Pilate.* This makes them agree;
But yet their friendship is my enmitie:
Was ever grief, &c.

Herod and all his bands do set me light,
Who teach all hands to warre, fingers to fight,
And onely am the Lord of hosts and might:
Was ever grief, &c.

Herod in judgement sits, while I do stand;
Examines me with a censorious hand:
I him obey, who all things else command:
Was ever grief like mine?

The *Jews* accuse me with despitefulnesse;
And vying malice with my gentlenesse,
Pick quarrels with their onely happinesse:
Was ever grief, &c.

I answer nothing, but with patience prove
If stonie hearts will melt with gentle love.
But who does hawk at eagles with a dove?
Was ever grief, &c.

My silence rather doth augment their crie;
My dove doth back into my bosome flie,
Because the raging waters still are high:
Was ever grief, &c.

Heark how they crie aloud still, *Crucifie:*
It is not fit he live a day, they crie,
Who cannot live lesse then eternally:
Was ever grief, &c.

Pilate a stranger holdeth off; but they,
Mine owne deare people, cry, *Away, away,*
With noises confused frighting the day:
Was ever grief, &c.

Yet still they shout, and crie, and stop their eares,
Putting my life among their sinnes and fears,
And therefore with *my bloud on them and theirs:*
Was ever grief, &c.

THE SACRIFICE

See how spite cankers things. These words aright
Used, and wished, are the whole worlds light:
But hony is their gall, brightnesse their night:
Was ever grief like mine?

They choose a murderer, and all agree
In him to do themselves a courtesie:
For it was their own cause who killed me:
Was ever grief, &c.

And a seditious murderer he was:
But I the Prince of peace; peace that doth passe
All understanding, more then heav'n doth glasse:
Was ever grief, &c.

Why, Cesar is their onely King, not I:
He clave the stonie rock, when they were drie;
But surely not their hearts, as I well trie:
Was ever grief, &c.

Ah! how they scourge me! yet my tendernesse
Doubles each lash: and yet their bitternesse
Windes up my grief to a mysteriousnesse:
Was ever grief, &c.

They buffet me, and box me as they list,
Who grasp the earth and heaven with my fist,
And never yet, whom I would punish, miss'd:
Was ever grief, &c.

Behold, they spit on me in scornfull wise,
Who by my spittle gave the blinde man eies,
Leaving his blindnesse to mine enemies:
Was ever grief, &c.

My face they cover, though it be divine.
As *Moses* face was vailed, so is mine,
Lest on their double-dark souls either shine :
Was ever grief like mine?

Servants and abjects flout me ; they are wittie :
Now prophesie who strikes thee, is their dittie.
So they in me denie themselves all pitie :
Was ever grief, &c.

And now I am deliver'd unto death,
Which each one cals for so with utmost breath,
That he before me well nigh suffereth :
Was ever grief, &c.

Weep not, deare friends, since I for both have wept
When all my tears were bloud, the while you slept :
Your tears for your own fortunes should be kept :
Was ever grief, &c.

The souldiers lead me to the common hall ;
There they deride me, they abuse me all :
Yet for twelve heav'nly legions I could call :
Was ever grief, &c.

Then with a scarlet robe they me aray ;
Which shews my bloud to be the onely way,
And cordiall left to repair mans decay :
Was ever grief, &c.

Then on my head a crown of thorns I wear :
For these are all the grapes *Sion* doth bear,
Though I my vine planted and watred there :
Was ever grief, &c.

THE SACRIFICE

So sits the earths great curse in *Adams* fall
Upon my head: so I remove it all
From th' earth unto my brows, and bear the thrall:
Was ever grief like mine?

Then with the reed they gave to me before,
They strike my head, the rock from whence all store
Of heav'nly blessings issue evermore:
Was ever grief, &c.

They bow their knees to me, and cry, *Hail king:*
What ever scoffes or scornfulnesse can bring,
I am the floore, the sink, where they it fling:
Was ever grief, &c.

Yet since mans scepters are as frail as reeds,
And thorny all their crowns, bloudie their weeds;
I, who am Truth, turn into truth their deeds:
Was ever grief, &c.

The souldiers also spit upon that face,
Which Angels did desire to have the grace,
And Prophets once to see, but found no place:
Was ever grief, &c.

Thus trimmed forth they bring me to the rout,
Who *Crucifie him*, crie with one strong shout.
God holds his peace at man, and man cries out:
Was ever grief, &c.

They leade me in once more, and putting then
Mine own clothes on, they leade me out agen.
Whom devils flie, thus is he toss'd of men:
Was ever grief, &c.

And now wearie of sport, glad to ingrosse
All spite in one, counting my life their losse,
They carrie me to my most bitter crosse:
Was ever grief like mine?

My crosse I bear my self, untill I faint:
Then Simon bears it for me by constraint,
The decreed burden of each mortall Saint:
Was ever grief, &c.

O all ye who passe by, behold and see;
Man stole the fruit, but I must climbe the tree;
The tree of life to all, but onely me:
Was ever grief, &c.

Lo, here I hang, charg'd with a world of sinne,
The greater world o' th' two; for that came in
By words, but this by sorrow I must win:
Was ever grief, &c.

Such sorrow, as if sinfull man could feel,
Or feel his part, he would not cease to kneel,
Till all were melted, though he were all steel:
Was ever grief, &c.

But, *O my God, my God!* why leav'st thou me,
The sonne, in whom thou dost delight to be?
My God, my God——
Never was grief like mine.

Shame tears my soul, my bodie many a wound;
Sharp nails pierce this, but sharper that confound;
Reproches, which are free, while I am bound.
Was ever grief, &c.

THE SACRIFICE

Now heal thy self, Physician; now come down.
Alas! I did so, when I left my crown
And fathers smile for you, to feel his frown:
Was ever grief like mine?

In healing not my self, there doth consist
All that salvation, which ye now resist;
Your safetie in my sicknesse doth subsist:
Was ever grief, &c.

Betwixt two theeves I spend my utmost breath,
As he that for some robberie suffereth.
Alas! what have I stollen from you? death:
Was ever grief, &c.

A king my title is, prefixt on high;
Yet by my subjects am condemn'd to die
A servile death in servile companie:
Was ever grief, &c.

They gave me vineger mingled with gall,
But more with malice: yet, when they did call,
With Manna, Angels food, I fed them all:
Was ever grief, &c.

They part my garments, and by lot dispose
My coat, the type of love, which once cur'd those
Who sought for help, never malicious foes:
Was ever grief, &c.

Nay, after death their spite shall further go;
For they will pierce my side, I full well know;
That as sinne came, so Sacraments might flow:
Was ever grief, &c.

But now I die; now all is finished.
My wo, mans weal: and now I bow my head.
Onely let others say, when I am dead,
Never was grief like mine.

THE THANKSGIVING

Oh King of grief! (a title strange, yet true,
To thee of all kings onely due)
Oh King of wounds! how shall I grieve for thee,
Who in all grief preventest me?
Shall I weep bloud? why thou hast wept such store
That all thy body was one doore.
Shall I be scourged, flouted, boxed, sold?
'Tis but to tell the tale is told.
My God, my God, why dost thou part from me?
Was such a grief as cannot be.
Shall I then sing, skipping, thy dolefull storie,
And side with thy triumphant glorie?
Shall thy strokes be my stroking? thorns, my flower?
Thy rod, my posie? crosse, my bower?
But how then shall I imitate thee, and
Copie thy fair, though bloudie hand?
Surely I will reuenge me on thy love,
And trie who shall victorious prove.
If thou dost give me wealth; I will restore
All back unto thee by the poore.
If thou dost give me honour; men shall see,
The honour doth belong to thee.
I will not marry; or, if she be mine,
She and her children shall be thine.

My bosome friend, if he blaspheme thy name,
    I will tear thence his lôve and fame.
One half of me being gone, the rest I give
    Unto some Chappell, die or live.
As for thy passion—But of that anon,
    When with the other I have done.
For thy predestination I'le contrive,
    That three yeares hence, if I survive,
I'le build a spittle, or mend common wayes,
    But mend mine own without delayes.
Then I will use the works of thy creation,
    As if I us'd them but for fashion.
The world and I will quarrell; and the yeare
    Shall not perceive, that I am here.
My musick shall finde thee, and ev'ry string
    Shall have his attribute to sing;
That all together may accord in thee,
    And prove one God, one harmonie.
If thou shalt give me wit, it shall appeare,
    If thou hast giv'n it me, 'tis here.
Nay, I will reade thy book, and never move
    Till I have found therein thy love;
Thy art of love, which I'le turn back on thee,
    O my deare Saviour, Victorie!
Then for thy passion—I will do for that—
    Alas, my God, I know not what.

THE REPRISALL

    I HAVE consider'd it, and finde
There is no dealing with thy mighty passion:
For though I die for thee, I am behinde;
    My sinnes deserve the condemnation.

O make me innocent, that I
May give a disentangled state and free:
And yet thy wounds still my attempts defie,
For by thy death I die for thee.

Ah! was it not enough that thou
By thy eternall glorie didst outgo me?
Couldst thou not griefs sad conquests me allow,
But in all vict'ries overthrow me?

Yet by confession will I come
Into the conquest. Though I can do nought
Against thee, in thee will I overcome
The man who once against thee fought.

THE AGONIE

PHILOSOPHERS have measur'd mountains,
Fathom'd the depths of seas, of states, and kings,
Walk'd with a staffe to heav'n, and traced fountains:
But there are two vast, spacious things,
The which to measure it doth more behove:
Yet few there are that found them; Sinne and Love.

Who would know Sinne, let him repair
Unto mount Olivet; there shall he see
A man so wrung with pains, that all his hair,
His skinne, his garments bloudie be.
Sinne is that presse and vice, which forceth pain
To hunt his cruell food through ev'ry vein.

GOOD FRIDAY

Who knows not Love, let him assay
And taste that juice, which on the crosse a pike
Did set again abroach ; then let him say
If ever he did taste the like.
Love is that liquour sweet and most divine,
Which my God feels as bloud ; but I, as wine.

THE SINNER

Lord, how I am all ague, when I seek
What I have treasur'd in my memorie !
Since, if my soul make even with the week,
Each seventh note by right is due to thee.
I finde there quarries of pil'd vanities,
But shreds of holinesse, that dare not venture
To shew their face, since crosse to thy decrees :
There the circumference earth is, heav'n the centre.
In so much dregs the quintessence is small :
The spirit and good extract of my heart
Comes to about the many hundredth part.
Yet Lord restore thine image, heare my call : [grone,
And though my hard heart scarce to thee can
Remember that thou once didst write in stone.

GOOD FRIDAY

O my chief good,
How shall I measure out thy bloud ?
How shall I count what thee befell,
And each grief tell ?

Shall I thy woes
Number according to thy foes?
Or, since one starre show'd thy first breath,
Shall all thy death?

Or shall each leaf,
Which falls in Autumne, score a grief?
Or cannot leaves, but fruit, be signe
Of the true vine?

Then let each houre
Of my whole life one grief devoure;
That thy distresse through all may runne,
And be my sunne.

Or rather let
My severall sinnes their sorrows get;
That as each beast his cure doth know,
Each sinne may so.

Since bloud is fittest, Lord, to write
Thy sorrows in, and bloudie fight;
My heart hath store, write there, where in
One box doth lie both ink and sinne:

That when sinne spies so many foes,
Thy whips, thy nails, thy wounds, thy woes,
All come to lodge there, sinne may say,
No room for me, and flie away.

Sinne being gone, oh fill the place,
And keep possession with thy grace;
Lest sinne take courage and return,
And all the writings blot or burn.

REDEMPTION

Having been tenant long to a rich Lord,
Not thriving, I resolved to be bold,
And make a suit unto him, to afford
A new small-rented lease, and cancell th' old.

In heaven at his manour I him sought:
They told me there, that he was lately gone
About some land, which he had dearly bought
Long since on earth, to take possession.

I straight return'd, and knowing his great birth,
Sought him accordingly in great resorts;
In cities, theatres, gardens, parks, and courts:
At length I heard a ragged noise and mirth

Of theeves and murderers: there I him espied,
Who straight, *Your suit is granted*, said, and died.

SEPULCHRE

O blessed bodie! Whither art thou thrown?
No lodging for thee, but a cold hard stone?
So many hearts on earth, and yet not one
Receive thee?

Sure there is room within our hearts good store;
For they can lodge transgressions by the score:
Thousands of toyes dwell there, yet out of doore
They leave thee.

But that which shews them large, shews them unfit.
What ever sinne did this pure rock commit,
Which holds thee now? Who hath indited it
Of murder?

Where our hard hearts have took up stones to brain thee,
And missing this, most falsly did arraigne thee;
Onely these stones in quiet entertain thee,
And order.

And as of old, the law by heav'nly art
Was writ in stone; so thou, which also art
The letter of the word, find'st no fit heart
To hold thee.

Yet do we still persist as we began,
And so should perish, but that nothing can,
Though it be cold, hard, foul, from loving man
Withold thee.

EASTER

Rise heart; thy Lord is risen. Sing his praise
Without delayes,
Who takes thee by the hand, that thou likewise
With him mayst rise:
That, as his death calcined thee to dust,
His life may make thee gold, and much more just.

EASTER

Awake, my lute, and struggle for thy part
With all thy art.
The crosse taught all wood to resound his name,
Who bore the same.
His streched sinews taught all strings, what key
Is best to celebrate this most high day.

Consort both heart and lute, and twist a song
Pleasant and long:
Or since all musick is but three parts vied
And multiplied;
O let thy blessed Spirit bear a part,
And make up our defects with his sweet art.

I got me flowers to straw thy way;
I got me boughs off many a tree:
But thou wast up by break of day,
And brought'st thy sweets along with thee.

The Sunne arising in the East,
Though he give light, & th' East perfume;
If they should offer to contest
With thy arising, they presume.

Can there be any day but this,
Though many sunnes to shine endeavour?
We count three hundred, but we misse:
There is but one, and that one ever.

EASTER WINGS

Lord, who createdst man in wealth and store,
Though foolishly he lost the same,
Decaying more and more,
Till he became
Most poore :
With thee
O let me rise
As larks, harmoniously,
And sing this day thy victories :
Then shall the fall further the flight in me.

EASTER WINGS

EASTER WINGS

My tender age in sorrow did beginne
And still with sicknesses and shame
Thou didst so punish sinne,
That I became
Most thinne.
With thee
Let me combine,
And feel this day thy victorie :
For, if I imp my wing on thine,
Affliction shall advance the flight in me.

H. BAPTISME

As he that sees a dark and shadie grove,
Stayes not, but looks beyond it on the skie;
So when I view my sinnes, mine eyes remove
More backward still, and to that water flie,

Which is above the heav'ns, whose spring and rent
Is in my deare Redeemers pierced side.
O blessed streams! either ye do prevent
And stop our sinnes from growing thick and wide,

Or else give tears to drown them, as they grow.
In you Redemption measures all my time,
And spreads the plaister equall to the crime:
You taught the book of life my name, that so

What ever future sinnes should me miscall,
Your first acquaintance might discredit all.

H. BAPTISME

Since, Lord, to thee
A narrow way and little gate
Is all the passage, on my infancie
Thou didst lay hold, and antedate
My faith in me.

O let me still
Write thee great God, and me a childe:
Let me be soft and supple to thy will,
Small to my self, to others milde,
Behither ill.

NATURE

Although by stealth
My flesh get on, yet let her sister
My soul bid nothing, but preserve her wealth:
The growth of flesh is but a blister;
Childhood is health.

NATURE

Full of rebellion, I would die,
Or fight, or travell, or denie
That thou hast ought to do with me.
O tame my heart;
It is thy highest art
To captivate strong holds to thee.

If thou shalt let this venome lurk,
And in suggestions fume and work,
My soul will turn to bubbles straight,
And thence by kinde
Vanish into a winde,
Making thy workmanship deceit.

O smooth my rugged heart, and there
Engrave thy rev'rend law and fear;
Or make a new one, since the old
Is saplesse grown,
And a much fitter stone
To hide my dust, then thee to hold.

SINNE

LORD, with what care hast thou begirt us round!
  Parents first season us: then schoolmasters
  Deliver us to laws; they send us bound
To rules of reason, holy messengers,

Pulpits and sundayes, sorrow dogging sinne,
  Afflictions sorted, anguish of all sizes,
  Fine nets and stratagems to catch us in,
Bibles laid open, millions of surprises,

Blessings beforehand, tyes of gratefulnesse,
  The sound of glorie ringing in our eares:
  Without, our shame; within, our consciences;
Angels and grace, eternall hopes and fears.

  Yet all these fences and their whole aray
  One cunning bosome-sinne blows quite away.

AFFLICTION

WHEN first thou didst entice to thee my heart,
      I thought the service brave:
So many joyes I writ down for my part,
      Besides what I might have
Out of my stock of naturall delights,
Augmented with thy gracious benefits.

AFFLICTION

I looked on thy furniture so fine,
　　　　　　　　And made it fine to me:
Thy glorious household-stuffe did me entwine,
　　　　　　　　And 'tice me unto thee.
Such starres I counted mine: both heav'n and earth
Payd me my wages in a world of mirth.

What pleasures could I want, whose King I served?
　　　　　　　　Where joyes my fellows were.
Thus argu'd into hopes, my thoughts reserved
　　　　　　　　No place for grief or fear.
Therefore my sudden soul caught at the place,
And made her youth and fiercenesse seek thy face.

At first thou gav'st me milk and sweetnesses;
　　　　　　　　I had my wish and way:
My dayes were straw'd with flow'rs and happinesse;
　　　　　　　　There was no moneth but May.
But with my yeares sorrow did twist and grow,
And made a partie unawares for wo.

My flesh began unto my soul in pain,
　　　　　　　　Sicknesses cleave my bones;
Consuming agues dwell in ev'ry vein,
　　　　　　　　And tune my breath to grones.
Sorrow was all my soul; I scarce beleeved,
Till grief did tell me roundly, that I lived.

When I got health, thou took'st away my life,
　　　　　　　　And more; for my friends die:
My mirth and age was lost; a blunted knife
　　　　　　　　Was of more use then I.
Thus thinne and lean without a fence or friend,
I was blown through with ev'ry storm and winde.

Whereas my birth and spirit rather took
                    The way that takes the town;
Thou didst betray me to a lingring book,
                    And wrap me in a gown.
I was entangled in the world of strife,
Before I had the power to change my life.

Yet, for I threatned oft the siege to raise,
                    Not simpring all mine age,
Thou often didst with Academick praise
                    Melt and dissolve my rage.
I took thy sweetned pill, till I came neare;
I could not go away, nor persevere.

Yet lest perchance I should too happie be
                    In my unhappinesse,
Turning my purge to food, thou throwest me
                    Into more sicknesses.
Thus doth thy power crosse-bias me, not making
Thine own gift good, yet me from my wayes taking.

Now I am here, what thou wilt do with me
                    None of my books will show:
I reade, and sigh, and wish I were a tree;
                    For sure then I should grow
To fruit or shade: at least some bird would trust
Her household to me, and I should be just.

Yet, though thou troublest me, I must be meek;
                    In weaknesse must be stout.
Well, I will change the service, and go seek
                    Some other master out.
Ah my deare God! though I am clean forgot,
Let me not love thee, if I love thee not.

REPENTANCE

REPENTANCE

Lord, I confesse my sinne is great;
Great is my sinne. Oh! gently treat
With thy quick flow'r, thy momentanie bloom;
Whose life still pressing
Is one undressing,
A steadie aiming at a tombe.

Mans age is two houres work, or three:
Each day doth round about us see.
Thus are we to delights: but we are all
To sorrows old,
If life be told
From what life feeleth, Adams fall.

O let thy height of mercie then
Compassionate short-breathed men.
Cut me not off for my most foul transgression:
I do confesse
My foolishnesse;
My God, accept of my confession.

Sweeten at length this bitter bowl,
Which thou hast pour'd into my soul;
Thy wormwood turn to health, windes to fair weather:
For if thou stay,
I and this day,
As we did rise, we die together.

When thou for sinne rebukest man,
Forthwith he waxeth wo and wan:
Bitternesse fills our bowels; all our hearts
Pine, and decay,
And drop away,
And carrie with them th' other parts.

But thou wilt sinne and grief destroy;
That so the broken bones may joy,
And tune together in a well-set song,
Full of his praises,
Who dead men raises.
Fractures well cur'd make us more strong.

FAITH

Lord, how couldst thou so much appease
Thy wrath for sinne, as when mans sight was dimme,
And could see little, to regard his ease,
And bring by Faith all things to him?

Hungrie I was, and had no meat:
I did conceit a most delicious feast;
I had it straight, and did as truly eat,
As ever did a welcome guest.

There is a rare outlandish root,
Which when I could not get, I thought it here:
That apprehension cur'd so well my foot,
That I can walk to heav'n well neare.

FAITH

I owed thousands and much more:
I did beleeve that I did nothing owe,
And liv'd accordingly; my creditor
Beleeves so too, and lets me go.

Faith makes me any thing, or all
That I beleeve is in the sacred storie:
And where sinne placeth me in Adams fall,
Faith sets me higher in his glorie.

If I go lower in the book,
What can be lower then the common manger?
Faith puts me there with him, who sweetly took
Our flesh and frailtie, death and danger.

If blisse had lien in art or strength,
None but the wise or strong had gained it:
Where now by Faith all arms are of a length;
One size doth all conditions fit.

A peasant may beleeve as much
As a great Clerk, and reach the highest stature.
Thus dost thou make proud knowledge bend & crouch
While grace fills up uneven nature.

When creatures had no reall light
Inherent in them, thou didst make the sunne,
Impute a lustre, and allow them bright;
And in this shew, what Christ hath done.

That which before was darkned clean
With bushie groves, pricking the lookers eie,
Vanisht away, when Faith did change the scene:
And then appear'd a glorious skie.

What though my bodie runne to dust?
Faith cleaves unto it, counting ev'ry grain
With an exact and most particular trust,
Reserving all for flesh again.

PRAYER

Prayer the Churches banquet, Angels age,
Gods breath in man returning to his birth,
The soul in paraphrase, heart in pilgrimage,
The Christian plummet sounding heav'n and earth;

Engine against th' Almightie, sinners towre,
Reversed thunder, Christ-side-piercing spear,
The six-daies—world transposing in an houre,
A kinde of tune, which all things heare and fear;

Softnesse, and peace, and joy, and love, and blisse,
Exalted Manna, gladnesse of the best,
Heaven in ordinarie, man well drest,
The milkie may, the bird of Paradise, [bloud,
Church-bels beyond the starres heard, the souls
The land of spices; something understood.

THE H. COMMUNION

Not in rich furniture, or fine aray,
Nor in a wedge of gold,
Thou, who from me wast sold,
To me dost now thy self convey;
For so thou should'st without me still have been,
Leaving within me sinne:

But by the way of nourishment and strength
Thou creep'st into my breast;
Making thy way my rest,
And thy small quantities my length;
Which spread their forces into every part,
Meeting sinnes force and art.

Yet can these not get over to my soul,
Leaping the wall that parts
Our souls and fleshly hearts;
But as th' outworks, they may controll
My rebel-flesh, and carrying thy name,
Affright both sinne and shame.

Onely thy grace, which with these elements comes,
Knoweth the ready way,
And hath the privie key,
Op'ning the souls most subtile rooms;
While those to spirits refin'd, at doore attend
Dispatches from their friend.

Give me my captive soul, or take
My bodie also thither.
Another lift like this will make
Them both to be together.

Before that sinne turn'd flesh to stone,
And all our lump to leaven;
A fervent sigh might well have blown
Our innocent earth to heaven.

For sure when Adam did not know
To sinne, or sinne to smother;
He might to heav'n from Paradise go,
As from one room t'another.

Thou hast restor'd us to this ease
By this thy heav'nly bloud;
Which I can go to, when I please,
And leave th' earth to their food.

ANTIPHON

Cho. Let all the world in ev'ry corner sing,
My God and King.

Vers. The heav'ns are not too high,
His praise may thither flie:
The earth is not too low,
His praises there may grow.

Cho. Let all the world in ev'ry corner sing,
My God and King.

Vers. The church with psalms must shout,
No doore can keep them out:
But above all, the heart
Must bear the longest part.

Cho. Let all the world in ev'ry corner sing,
My God and King.

LOVE

I

Immortall Love, authour of this great frame,
Sprung from that beautie which can never fade;
How hath man parcel'd out thy glorious name,
And thrown it on that dust which thou hast made,

While mortall love doth all the title gain!
Which siding with invention, they together
Bear all the sway, possessing heart and brain,
(Thy workmanship) and give thee share in neither.

Wit fancies beautie, beautie raiseth wit:
The world is theirs; they two play out the game,
Thou standing by: and though thy glorious name
Wrought out deliverance from th' infernall pit,

Who sings thy praise? onely a skarf or glove
Doth warm our hands, and make them write of love.

II

IMMORTALL Heat, O let thy greater flame
Attract the lesser to it: let those fires,
Which shall consume the world, first make it tame;
And kindle in our hearts such true desires,

As may consume our lusts, and make thee way. [brain
Then shall our hearts pant thee; then shall our
All her invention on thine Altar lay,
And there in hymnes send back thy fire again:

Our eies shall see thee, which before saw dust;
Dust blown by wit, till that they both were blinde:
Thou shalt recover all thy goods in kinde,
Who wert disseized by usurping lust:

All knees shall bow to thee; all wits shall rise,
And praise him who did make and mend our eies.

THE TEMPER

How should I praise thee, Lord! how should my
Gladly engrave thy love in steel, [rymes
If what my soul doth feel sometimes,
My soul might ever feel!

Although there were some fourtie heav'ns, or more,
Sometimes I peere above them all;
Sometimes I hardly reach a score,
Sometimes to hell I fall.

O rack me not to such a vast extent;
Those distances belong to thee:
The world's too little for thy tent,
A grave too big for me.

Wilt thou meet arms with man, that thou dost stretch
A crumme of dust from heav'n to hell?
Will great God measure with a wretch?
Shall he thy stature spell?

O let me, when thy roof my soul hath hid,
O let me roost and nestle there:
Then of a sinner thou art rid,
And I of hope and fear.

Yet take thy way; for sure thy way is best:
Stretch or contract me thy poore debter:
This is but tuning of my breast,
To make the musick better.

Whether I flie with angels, fall with dust,
Thy hands made both, and I am there :
Thy power and love, my love and trust
Make one place ev'ry where.

THE TEMPER

It cannot be. Where is that mightie joy,
Which just now took up all my heart ?
Lord, if thou must needs use thy dart,
Save that, and me ; or sin for both destroy.

The grosser world stands to thy word and art ;
But thy diviner world of grace
Thou suddenly dost raise and race,
And ev'ry day a new Creatour art.

O fix thy chair of grace, that all my powers
May also fix their reverence :
For when thou dost depart from hence,
They grow unruly, and sit in thy bowers.

Scatter, or binde them all to bend to thee :
Though elements change, and heaven move,
Let not thy higher Court remove,
But keep a standing Majestie in me.

JORDAN

Who sayes that fictions onely and false hair
Become a verse? Is there in truth no beautie?
Is all good structure in a winding stair?
May no lines passe, except they do their dutie
  Not to a true, but painted chair?

Is it no verse, except enchanted groves
And sudden arbours shadow course-spunne lines?
Must purling streams refresh a lovers loves?
Must all be vail'd, while he that reades, divines,
  Catching the sense at two removes?

Shepherds are honest people; let them sing:
Riddle who list, for me, and pull for Prime:
I envie no mans nightingale or spring;
Nor let them punish me with losse of ryme,
  Who plainly say, *My God, My King.*

EMPLOYMENT

If as a flowre doth spread and die,
Thou wouldst extend me to some good,
Before I were by frosts extremitie
  Nipt in the bud;

The sweetnesse and the praise were thine;
But the extension and the room,
Which in thy garland I should fill, were mine
  At thy great doom.

For as thou dost impart thy grace,
The greater shall our glorie be.
The measure of our joyes is in this place,
The stuffe with thee.

Let me not languish then, and spend
A life as barren to thy praise,
As is the dust, to which that life doth tend,
But with delaies.

All things are busie; onely I
Neither bring hony with the bees,
Nor flowres to make that, nor the husbandrie
To water these.

I am no link of thy great chain,
But all my companie is a weed.
Lord place me in thy comfort; give one strain
To my poore reed.

THE H. SCRIPTURES

I

Oh Book! infinite sweetnesse! let my heart
Suck ev'ry letter, and a hony gain,
Precious for any grief in any part;
To cleare the breast, to mollifie all pain.

Thou art all health, health thriving, till it make
A full eternitie: thou art a masse
Of strange delights, where we may wish and take.
Ladies, look here; this is the thankfull glasse,

That mends the lookers eyes: this is the well
  That washes what it shows. Who can indeare
  Thy praise too much? thou art heav'ns Lidger
Working against the states of death and hell. [here,

  Thou art joyes handsell: heav'n lies flat in thee,
  Subject to ev'ry mounters bended knee.

II

Oh that I knew how all thy lights combine,
  And the configurations of their glorie!
  Seeing not onely how each verse doth shine,
But all the constellations of the storie.

This verse marks that, and both do make a motion
  Unto a third, that ten leaves off doth lie:
  Then as dispersed herbs do watch a potion,
These three make up some Christians destinie:

Such are thy secrets, which my life makes good,
  And comments on thee: for in ev'ry thing
  Thy words do finde me out, and parallels bring,
And in another make me understood.

  Starres are poore books, and oftentimes do misse:
  This book of starres lights to eternall blisse.

WHITSUNDAY

  Listen sweet Dove unto my song,
  And spread thy golden wings in me;
  Hatching my tender heart so long,
Till it get wing, and flie away with thee.

WHITSUNDAY

Where is that fire which once descended
On thy Apostles? thou didst then
Keep open house, richly attended,
Feasting all comers by twelve chosen men.

Such glorious gifts thou didst bestow,
That th' earth did like a heav'n appeare;
The starres were coming down to know
If they might mend their wages, and serve here.

The sunne, which once did shine alone,
Hung down his head, and wisht for night,
When he beheld twelve sunnes for one
Going about the world, and giving light.

But since those pipes of gold, which brought
That cordiall water to our ground,
Were cut and martyr'd by the fault
Of those, who did themselves through their side wound.

Thou shutt'st the doore, and keep'st within;
Scarce a good joy creeps through the chink:
And if the braves of conqu'ring sinne
Did not excite thee, we should wholly sink.

Lord, though we change, thou art the same;
The same sweet God of love and light:
Restore this day, for thy great name,
Unto his ancient and miraculous right.

GRACE

My stock lies dead, and no increase
Doth my dull husbandrie improve:
O let thy graces without cease
Drop from above!

If still the sunne should hide his face,
Thy house would but a dungeon prove,
Thy works nights captives: O let grace
Drop from above!

The dew doth ev'ry morning fall;
And shall the dew out-strip thy dove?
The dew, for which grasse cannot call,
Drop from above.

Death is still working like a mole,
And digs my grave at each remove:
Let grace work too, and on my soul
Drop from above.

Sinne is still hammering my heart
Unto a hardnesse, void of love:
Let suppling grace, to crosse his art,
Drop from above.

O come! for thou dost know the way.
Or if to me thou wilt not move,
Remove me, where I need not say,
Drop from above.

PRAISE

To write a verse or two, is all the praise,
That I can raise:
Mend my estate in any wayes,
Thou shalt have more.

I go to Church; help me to wings, and I
Will thither flie;
Or, if I mount unto the skie,
I will do more.

Man is all weaknesse; there is no such thing
As Prince or King:
His arm is short; yet with a sling
He may do more.

An herb destill'd, and drunk, may dwell next doore,
On the same floore,
To a brave soul: Exalt the poore,
They can do more.

O raise me then! poore bees, that work all day,
Sting my delay,
Who have a work, as well as they,
And much, much more.

AFFLICTION

Kill me not ev'ry day,
Thou Lord of life; since thy one death for me
Is more then all my deaths can be,
Though I in broken pay
Die over each houre of Methusalems stay.

If all mens tears were let
Into one common sewer, sea, and brine ;
What were they all, compar'd to thine ?
Wherein if they were set,
They would discolour thy most bloudy sweat.

Thou art my grief alone,
Thou Lord conceal it not : and as thou art
All my delight, so all my smart :
Thy crosse took up in one,
By way of imprest, all my future mone.

MATTENS

I CANNOT ope mine eyes,
But thou art ready there to catch
My morning-soul and sacrifice :
Then we must needs for that day make a match.

My God, what is a heart ?
Silver, or gold, or precious stone,
Or starre, or rainbow, or a part
Of all these things, or all of them in one ?

My God, what is a heart,
That thou shouldst it so eye, and wooe,
Powring upon it all thy art,
As if that thou hadst nothing els to do ?

Indeed mans whole estate
Amounts (and richly) to serve thee :
He did not heav'n and earth create,
Yet studies them, not him by whom they be

Teach me thy love to know;
That this new light, which now I see,
May both the work and workman show:
Then by a sunne-beam I will climbe to thee.

SINNE

O THAT I could a sinne once see!
We paint the devil foul, yet he
Hath some good in him, all agree.
Sinne is flat opposite to th' Almighty, seeing
It wants the good of *vertue*, and of *being*.

But God more care of us hath had:
If apparitions make us sad,
By sight of sinne we should grow mad.
Yet as in sleep we see foul death, and live:
So devils are our sinnes in perspective.

EVEN-SONG

BLEST be the God of love,
Who gave me eyes, and light, and power this day,
Both to be busie, and to play.
But much more blest be God above,

Who gave me sight alone,
Which to himself he did denie:
For when he sees my waies, I dy:
But I have got his sonne, and he hath none.

What have I brought thee home
For this thy love? have I discharg'd the debt,
Which this dayes favour did beget?
I ranne; but all I brought, was fome.

Thy diet, care, and cost
Do end in bubbles, balls of winde;
Of winde to thee whom I have crost,
But balls of wilde-fire to my troubled minde.

Yet still thou goest on,
And now with darknesse closest wearie eyes,
Saying to man, *It doth suffice:*
Henceforth repose; your work is done.

Thus in thy Ebony box
Thou dost enclose us, till the day
Put our amendment in our way,
And give new wheels to our disorder'd clocks.

I muse, which shows more love,
The day or night: that is the gale, this th' harbour;
That is the walk, and this the arbour;
Or that the garden, this the grove.

My God, thou art all love.
Not one poore minute 'scapes thy breast,
But brings a favour from above;
And in this love, more then in bed, I rest.

CHURCH-MONUMENTS

While that my soul repairs to her devotion,
Here I entombe my flesh, that it betimes
May take acquaintance of this heap of dust;
To which the blast of deaths incessant motion,
Fed with the exhalation of our crimes,
Drives all at last. Therefore I gladly trust

My bodie to this school, that it may learn
To spell his elements, and finde his birth
Written in dustie heraldrie and lines;
Which dissolution sure doth best discern,
Comparing dust with dust, and earth with earth.
These laugh at Ieat, and Marble put for signes,

To sever the good fellowship of dust,
And spoil the meeting. What shall point out them,
When they shall bow, and kneel, and fall down flat
To kisse those heaps, which now they have in trust?
Deare flesh, while I do pray, learn here thy stemme
And true descent; that when thou shalt grow fat,

And wanton in thy cravings, thou mayst know,
That flesh is but the glasse, which holds the dust
That measures all our time; which also shall
Be crumbled into dust. Mark here below
How tame these ashes are, how free from lust,
That thou mayst fit thy self against thy fall.

CHURCH-MUSICK

Sweetest of sweets, I thank you: when displeasure
Did through my bodie wound my minde,
You took me thence, and in your house of pleasure
A daintie lodging me assign'd.

Now I in you without a bodie move,
Rising and falling with your wings:
We both together sweetly live and love,
Yet say sometimes, *God help poore Kings*.

Comfort, 'Ile die; for if you poste from me,
Sure I shall do so, and much more:
But if I travell in your companie,
You know the way to heavens doore.

CHURCH-LOCK AND KEY

I know it is my sinne, which locks thine eares,
And bindes thy hands;
Out-crying my requests, drowning my tears;
Or else the chilnesse of my faint demands.

But as cold hands are angrie with the fire,
And mend it still;
So I do lay the want of my desire,
Not on my sinnes, or coldnesse, but thy will.

Yet heare, O God, onely for his bloods sake
Which pleads for me:
For though sinnes plead too, yet like stones they make
His bloods sweet current much more loud to be.

THE CHURCH-FLOORE

MARK you the floore? that square and speckled stone,
Which looks so firm and strong,
Is *Patience*:

And th' other black and grave, wherewith each one
Is checker'd all along,
Humilitie:

The gentle rising, which on either hand
Leads to the Quire above,
Is *Confidence*:

But the sweet cement, which in one sure band
Ties the whole frame, is *Love*
And *Charitie*.

Hither sometimes Sinne steals, and stains
The marbles neat and curious veins:
But all is cleansed when the marble weeps.
Sometimes Death, puffing at the doore,
Blows all the dust about the floore:
But while he thinks to spoil the room, he sweeps.
Blest be the *Architect*, whose art
Could build so strong in a weak heart.

THE WINDOWS

LORD, how can man preach thy eternall word?
He is a brittle crazie glasse:
Yet in thy temple thou dost him afford
This glorious and transcendent place,
To be a window, through thy grace.

But when thou dost anneal in glasse thy storie,
Making thy life to shine within
The holy Preachers; then the light and glorie
More rev'rend grows, and more doth win:
Which else shows watrish, bleak, and thin.

Doctrine and life, colours and light, in one
When they combine and mingle, bring
A strong regard and aw: but speech alone
Doth vanish like a flaring thing,
And in the eare, not conscience ring.

TRINITIE SUNDAY

Lord, who hast form'd me out of mud,
And hast redeem'd me through thy bloud,
And sanctifi'd me to do good;

Purge all my sinnes done heretofore:
For I confesse my heavie score,
And I will strive to sinne no more.

Enrich my heart, mouth, hands in me,
With faith, with hope, with charitie;
That I may runne, rise, rest with thee.

CONTENT

Peace mutt'ring thoughts, and do not grudge to keep
Within the walls of your own breast:
Who cannot on his own bed sweetly sleep,
Can on anothers hardly rest.

CONTENT

Gad not abroad at ev'ry quest and call
Of an untrained hope or passion.
To court each place or fortune that doth fall,
Is wantonnesse in contemplation.

Mark how the fire in flints doth quiet lie,
Content and warm t' it self alone:
But when it would appeare to others eye,
Without a knock it never shone.

Give me the pliant minde, whose gentle measure
Complies and suits with all estates;
Which can let loose to a crown, and yet with pleasure
Take up within a cloisters gates.

This soul doth span the world, and hang content
From either pole unto the centre:
Where in each room of the well-furnisht tent
He lies warm, and without adventure.

The brags of life are but a nine dayes wonder;
And after death the fumes that spring
From private bodies, make as big a thunder,
As those which rise from a huge King.

Onely thy Chronicle is lost; and yet
Better by worms be all once spent,
Then to have hellish moths still gnaw and fret
Thy name in books, which may not rent:

When all thy deeds, whose brunt thou feel'st alone,
Are chaw'd by others pens and tongues;
And as their wit is, their digestion,
Thy nourisht fame is weak or strong.

Then cease discoursing soul, till thine own ground,
Do not thy self or friends importune.
He that by seeking hath himself once found,
Hath euer found a happie fortune.

THE QUIDDITIE

My God, a verse is not a crown,
No point of honour, or gay suit,
No hawk, or banquet, or renown,
Nor a good sword, nor yet a lute:

It cannot vault, or dance, or play;
It never was in *France* or *Spain*;
Nor can it entertain the day
With a great stable or demain:

It is no office, art, or news,
Nor the Exchange, or busie Hall;
But it is that which while I use
I am with thee, and *Most take all*.

HUMILITIE

I saw the vertues sitting hand in hand
In sev'rall ranks upon an azure throne,
Where all the beasts and fowls by their command
Presented tokens of submission.
Humilitie, who sat the lowest there
To execute their call,
When by the beasts the presents tendred were,
Gave them about to all.

The angrie Lion did present his paw,
Which by consent was giv'n to Mansuetude.
The fearfull Hare her eares, which by their law
Humilitie did reach to Fortitude.
The jealous Turkie brought his corall-chain;
That went to Temperance.
On Justice was bestow'd the Foxes brain,
Kill'd in the way by chance.

At length the Crow bringing the Peacocks plume,
(For he would not) as they beheld the grace
Of that brave gift, each one began to fume,
And challenge it, as proper to his place,
Till they fell out: which when the beasts espied,
They leapt upon the throne;
And if the Fox had liv'd to rule their side,
They had depos'd each one.

Humilitie, who held the plume, at this
Did weep so fast, that the tears trickling down
Spoil'd all the train: then saying, *Here it is*
For which ye wrangle, made them turn their frown
Against the beasts: so joyntly bandying,
They drive them soon away;
And then amerc'd them, double gifts to bring
At the next Session-day.

FRAILTIE

LORD, in my silence how do I despise
What upon trust
Is styled *honour*, *riches*, or *fair eyes*;
But is *fair dust*!

I surname them *guilded clay*,
Deare earth, *fine grasse* or *hay*;
In all, I think my foot doth ever tread
Upon their head.

But when I view abroad both Regiments;
The worlds, and thine:
Thine clad with simplenesse, and sad events;
The other fine,
Full of glorie and gay weeds,
Brave language, braver deeds:
That which was dust before, doth quickly rise,
And prick mine eyes.

O brook not this, lest if what even now
My foot did tread,
Affront those joyes, wherewith thou didst endow,
And long since wed
My poore soul, ev'n sick of love:
It may a Babel prove.
Commodious to conquer heav'n and thee
Planted in me.

CONSTANCIE

Who is the honest man?
He that doth still and strongly good pursue,
To God, his neighbour, and himself most true:
Whom neither force nor fawning can
Unpinne, or wrench from giving all their due.

Whose honestie is not
So loose or easie, that a ruffling winde
Can blow away, or glittering look it blinde:
Who rides his sure and even trot,
While the world now rides by, now lags behinde.

Who, when great trials come,
Nor seeks, nor shunnes them; but doth calmly stay,
Till he the thing and the example weigh:
All being brought into a summe,
What place or person calls for, he doth pay.

Whom none can work or wooe
To use in any thing a trick or sleight,
For above all things he abhorres deceit:
His words and works and fashion too
All of a piece, and all are cleare and straight.

Who never melts or thaws
At close tentations: when the day is done,
His goodnesse sets not, but in dark can runne:
The sunne to others writeth laws,
And is their vertue; Vertue is his Sunne.

Who, when he is to treat
With sick folks, women, those whom passions sway,
Allows for that, and keeps his constant way:
Whom others faults do not defeat;
But though men fail him, yet his part doth play.

Whom nothing can procure,
When the wide world runnes bias, from his will
To writhe his limbes, and share, not mend the ill.
This is the Mark-man, safe and sure,
Who still is right, and prayes to be so still.

AFFLICTION

My heart did heave, and there came forth, *O God!*
By that I knew that thou wast in the grief,
To guide and govern it to my relief,
        Making a sceptre of the rod:
            Hadst thou not had thy part,
Sure the unruly sigh had broke my heart.

But since thy breath gave me both life and shape,
Thou knowst my tallies; and when there's assign'd
So much breath to a sigh, what's then behinde?
        Or if some yeares with it escape,
            The sigh then onely is
A gale to bring me sooner to my blisse.

Thy life on earth was grief, and thou art still
Constant unto it, making it to be
A point of honour, now to grieve in me,
        And in thy members suffer ill.
            They who lament one crosse,
Thou dying dayly, praise thee to thy losse.

THE STARRE

Bright spark, shot from a brighter place,
    Where beams surround my Saviours face,
        Canst thou be any where
            So well as there?

Yet, if thou wilt from thence depart,
Take a bad lodging in my heart;
For thou canst make a debter,
And make it better.

First with thy fire-work burn to dust
Folly, and worse then folly, lust:
Then with thy light refine,
And make it shine:

So disengag'd from sinne and sicknesse,
Touch it with thy celestiall quicknesse,
That it may hang and move
After thy love.

Then with our trinitie of light,
Motion, and heat, let's take our flight
Unto the place where thou
Before didst bow.

Get me a standing there, and place
Among the beams, which crown the face
Of him, who dy'd to part
Sinne and my heart:

That so among the rest I may
Glitter, and curle, and winde as they:
That winding is their fashion
Of adoration.

Sure thou wilt joy, by gaining me
To flie home like a laden bee
Unto that hive of beams
And garland-streams.

SUNDAY

O DAY most calm, most bright,
The fruit of this, the next worlds bud,
Th' indorsement of supreme delight,
Writ by a friend, and with his bloud;
The couch of time; cares balm and bay:
The week were dark, but for thy light:
Thy torch doth show the way.

The other dayes and thou
Make up one man; whose face thou art,
Knocking at heaven with thy brow:
The worky-daies are the back-part;
The burden of the week lies there,
Making the whole to stoup and bow,
Till thy release appeare.

Man had straight forward gone
To endlesse death: but thou dost pull
And turn us round to look on one,
Whom, if we were not very dull,
We could not choose but look on still;
Since there is no place so alone,
The which he doth not fill.

Sundaies the pillars are,
On which heav'ns palace arched lies:
The other dayes fill up the spare
And hollow room with vanities.
They are the fruitfull beds and borders
In Gods rich garden: that is bare,
Which parts their ranks and orders.

SUNDAY

The Sundaies of mans life,
Thredded together on times string,
Make bracelets to adorn the wife
Of the eternall glorious King.
On Sunday heavens gate stands ope;
Blessings are plentifull and rife,
More plentifull then hope.

This day my Saviour rose,
And did inclose this light for his:
That, as each beast his manger knows,
Man might not of his fodder misse.
Christ hath took in this piece of ground,
And made a garden there for those
Who want herbs for their wound.

The rest of our Creation
Our great Redeemer did remove
With the same shake, which at his passion
Did th' earth and all things with it move.
As Samson bore the doores away,
Christs hands, though nail'd, wrought our salvation,
And did unhinge that day.

The brightnesse of that day
We sullied by our foul offence:
Wherefore that robe we cast away,
Having a new at his expence,
Whose drops of bloud paid the full price,
That was requir'd to make us gay,
And fit for Paradise.

Thou art a day of mirth :
And where the week-dayes trail on ground,
Thy flight is higher, as thy birth.
O let me take thee at the bound,
Leaping with thee from sev'n to sev'n,
Till that we both, being toss'd from earth,
Flie hand in hand to heav'n !

AVARICE

Money, thou bane of blisse, and sourse of wo,
Whence com'st thou, that thou art so fresh and fine?
I know thy parentage is base and low :
Man found thee poore and dirtie in a mine.

Surely thou didst so little contribute
To this great kingdome, which thou now hast got,
That he was fain, when thou wert destitute,
To digge thee out of thy dark cave and grot :

Then forcing thee, by fire he made thee bright :
Nay, thou hast got the face of man ; for we
Have with our stamp and seal transferr'd our right :
Thou art the man, and man but drosse to thee.

Man calleth thee his wealth, who made thee rich ;
And while he digs out thee, falls in the ditch.

Ana- { Mary / Army } *gram*

How well her name an *Army* doth present,
In whom the *Lord of hosts* did pitch his tent !

TO ALL ANGELS AND SAINTS

Oh glorious spirits, who after all your bands
See the smooth face of God, without a frown
Or strict commands;
Where ev'ry one is king, and hath his crown,
If not upon his head, yet in his hands:

Not out of envie or maliciousnesse
Do I forbear to crave your speciall aid:
I would addresse
My vows to thee most gladly, blessed Maid,
And Mother of my God, in my distresse.

Thou art the holy mine, whence came the gold,
The great restorative for all decay
In young and old;
Thou art the cabinet where the jewell lay:
Chiefly to thee would I my soul unfold:

But now (alas!) I dare not; for our King,
Whom we do all joyntly adore and praise,
Bids no such thing:
And where his pleasure no injunction layes,
('Tis your own case) ye never move a wing.

All worship is prerogative, and a flower
Of his rich crown, from whom lyes no appeal
At the last houre:
Therefore we dare not from his garland steal,
To make a posie for inferiour power.

Although then others court you, if ye know
What's done on earth, we shall not fare the worse,
Who do not so;
Since we are ever ready to disburse,
If any one our Masters hand can show.

EMPLOYMENT

He that is weary, let him sit.
My soul would stirre
And trade in courtesies and wit,
Quitting the furre
To cold complexions needing it.

Man is no starre, but a quick coal
Of mortall fire:
Who blows it not, nor doth controll
A faint desire,
Lets his own ashes choke his soul.

When th' elements did for place contest
With him, whose will
Ordain'd the highest to be best;
The earth sat still,
And by the others is opprest.

Life is a businesse, not good cheer;
Ever in warres.
The sunne still shineth there or here,
Whereas the starres
Watch an advantage to appeare.

Oh that I were an Orenge-tree,
That busie plant!
Then should I ever laden be,
And never want
Some fruit for him that dressed me.

But we are still too young or old;
The man is gone,
Before we do our wares unfold:
So we freeze on,
Until the grave increase our cold.

DENIALL

When my devotions could not pierce
Thy silent eares;
Then was my heart broken, as was my verse:
My breast was full of fears
And disorder:

My bent thoughts, like a brittle bow,
Did flie asunder:
Each took his way; some would to pleasures go,
Some to the warres and thunder
Of alarms.

As good go any where, they say,
As to benumme
Both knees and heart, in crying night and day,
Come, come, my God, O come,
But no hearing.

O that thou shouldst give dust a tongue
To crie to thee,
And then not heare it crying! all day long
My heart was in my knee,
But no hearing.

Therefore my soul lay out of sight,
Untun'd, unstrung:
My feeble spirit, unable to look right,
Like a nipt blossome, hung
Discontented.

O cheer and tune my heartlesse breast,
Deferre no time;
That so thy favours granting my request,
They and my minde may chime,
And mend my ryme.

CHRISTMAS

ALL after pleasures as I rid one day,
My horse and I, both tir'd, bodie and minde,
With full crie of affections, quite astray;
I took up in the next inne I could finde.

There when I came, whom found I but my deare,
My dearest Lord, expecting till the grief
Of pleasures brought me to him, readie there
To be all passengers most sweet relief?

O Thou, whose glorious, yet contracted light,
Wrapt in nights mantle, stole into a manger;
Since my dark soul and brutish is thy right,
To Man of all beasts be not thou a stranger:

Furnish and deck my soul, that thou mayst have
A better lodging, then a rack, or grave.

THE shepherds sing; and shall I silent be?
My God, no hymne for thee?
My soul's a shepherd too; a flock it feeds
Of thoughts, and words, and deeds.
The pasture is thy word: the streams, thy grace
Enriching all the place.
Shepherd and flock shall sing, and all my powers
Out-sing the day-light houres.
Then we will chide the sunne for letting night
Take up his place and right:
We sing one common Lord; wherefore he should
Himself the candle hold.
I will go searching, till I finde a sunne
Shall stay, till we have done;
A willing shiner, that shall shine as gladly,
As frost-nipt sunnes look sadly.
Then we will sing, and shine all our own day,
And one another pay:
His beams shall cheer my breast, and both so twine,
Till ev'n his beams sing, and my musick shine.

UNGRATEFULNESSE

LORD, with what bountie and rare clemencie
Hast thou redeem'd us from the grave!
If thou hadst let us runne,
Gladly had man ador'd the sunne,
And thought his god most brave;
Where now we shall be better gods then he.

Thou hast but two rare cabinets full of treasure,
The *Trinitie*, and *Incarnation:*
Thou hast unlockt them both,
And made them jewels to betroth
The work of thy creation
Unto thy self in everlasting pleasure.

The statelier cabinet is the *Trinitie*,
Whose sparkling light accesse denies:
Therefore thou dost not show
This fully to us, till death blow
The dust into our eyes:
For by that powder thou wilt make us see.

But all thy sweets are packt up in the other;
Thy mercies thither flock and flow:
That as the first affrights,
This may allure us with delights;
Because this box we know;
For we have all of us just such another.

But man is close, reserv'd, and dark to thee:
When thou demandest but a heart,
He cavils instantly.
In his poore cabinet of bone
Sinnes have their box apart,
Defrauding thee, who gavest two for one.

SIGHS AND GRONES

O do not use me
After my sinnes! look not on my desert,
But on thy glorie! then thou wilt reform
And not refuse me: for thou onely art
The mightie God, but I a sillie worm;
O do not bruise me!

O do not urge me!
For what account can thy ill steward make?
I have abus'd thy stock, destroy'd thy woods,
Suckt all thy magazens: my head did ake,
Till it found out how to consume thy goods:
O do not scourge me!

O do not blinde me!
I have deserv'd that an Egyptian night
Should thicken all my powers; because my lust
Hath still sow'd fig-leaves to exclude thy light:
But I am frailtie, and already dust;
O do not grinde me!

O do not fill me
With the turn'd viall of thy bitter wrath!
For thou hast other vessels full of bloud,
A part whereof my Saviour empti'd hath,
Ev'n unto death: since he di'd for my good,
O do not kill me!

But O reprieve me!
For thou hast *life* and *death* at thy command;
Thou art both *Judge* and *Saviour*, *feast* and *rod*,
Cordiall and *Corrosive*: put not thy hand
Into the bitter box; but O my God,
My God, relieve me!

THE WORLD

Love built a stately house; where *Fortune* came,
And spinning phansies, she was heard to say,
That her fine cobwebs did support the frame,
Whereas they were supported by the same:
But *Wisdome* quickly swept them all away.

Then *Pleasure* came, who liking not the fashion,
Began to make *Balcones, Terraces,*
Till she had weakened all by alteration:
But rev'rend *laws*, and many a *proclamation*
Reformed all at length with menaces.

Then enter'd *Sinne*, and with that Sycomore,
Whose leaves first sheltred man from drought and dew,
Working and winding slily evermore,
The inward walls and Sommers cleft and tore:
But *Grace* shor'd these, and cut that as it grew.

Then *Sinne* combin'd with *Death* in a firm band
To rase the building to the very floore:
Which they effected, none could them withstand,
But *Love* and *Grace* took *Glorie* by the hand,
And built a braver Palace then before.

COLOSS. III. 3

Our life is hid with Christ in God.

My words & thoughts do both expresse this notion,
That *Life* hath with the sun a double motion.
The first *Is* straight, and our diurnall friend,
The other *Hid*, and doth obliquely bend.
One life is wrapt *In* flesh, and tends to earth.
The other winds towards *Him*, whose happie birth
Taught me to live here so, *That* still one eye
Should aim and shoot at that which *Is* on high:
Quitting with daily labour all *My* pleasure,
To gain at harvest an eternall *Treasure*.

VANITIE

THE fleet Astronomer can bore,
And thred the spheres with his quick-piercing minde:
He views their stations, walks from doore to doore,
Surveys, as if he had design'd
To make a purchase there: he sees their dances,
And knoweth long before,
Both their full-ey'd aspects, and secret glances.

The nimble Diver with his side
Cuts through the working waves, that he may fetch
His dearely-earned pearl, which God did hide
On purpose from the ventrous wretch;
That he might save his life, and also hers,
Who with excessive pride
Her own destruction and his danger wears.

The subtil Chymick can devest
And strip the creature naked, till he finde
The callow principles within their nest:
There he imparts to them his minde,
Admitted to their bed-chamber, before
They appeare trim and drest
To ordinarie suitours at the doore.

What hath not man sought out and found,
But his deare God? who yet his glorious law
Embosomes in us, mellowing the ground
With showres and frosts, with love & aw,
So that we need not say, Where's this command?
Poore man, thou searchest round
To finde out *death*, but missest *life* at hand.

LENT

WELCOME deare feast of Lent: who loves not thee,
He loves not Temperance, or Authoritie,
But is compos'd of passion.
The Scriptures bid us *fast;* the Church sayes, *now:*
Give to thy Mother, what thou wouldst allow
To ev'ry Corporation.

The humble soul compos'd of love and fear
Begins at home, and layes the burden there,
When doctrines disagree
He sayes, in things which use hath justly got,
I am a scandall to the Church, and not
The Church is so to me.

True Christians should be glad of an occasion
To use their temperance, seeking no evasion,
When good is seasonable;
Unlesse Authoritie, which should increase
The obligation in us, make it lesse,
And Power it self disable.

Besides the cleannesse of sweet abstinence,
Quick thoughts and motions at a small expense,
A face not fearing light:
Whereas in fulnesse there are sluttish fumes,
Sowre exhalations, and dishonest rheumes,
Revenging the delight.

Then those same pendant profits, which the spring
And Easter intimate, enlarge the thing,
And goodnesse of the deed.
Neither ought other mens abuse of Lent
Spoil the good use; lest by that argument
We forfeit all our Creed.

It's true, we cannot reach Christs forti'th day;
Yet to go part of that religious way,
Is better then to rest:
We cannot reach our Saviours puritie;
Yet are we bid, *Be holy ev'n as he.*
In both let's do our best.

Who goeth in the way which Christ hath gone,
Is much more sure to meet with him, then one
That travelleth by-wayes:
Perhaps my God, though he be farre before,
May turn, and take me by the hand, and more
May strengthen my decayes.

Yet Lord instruct us to improve our fast
By starving sinne and taking such repast,
As may our faults controll:
That ev'ry man may revell at his doore,
Not in his parlour; banquetting the poore,
And among those his soul.

VERTUE

Sweet day, so cool, so calm, so bright,
The bridall of the earth and skie:
The dew shall weep thy fall to night;
For thou must die.

Sweet rose, whose hue angrie and brave
Bids the rash gazer wipe his eye:
Thy root is ever in its grave,
And thou must die.

Sweet spring, full of sweet dayes and roses,
A box where sweets compacted lie;
My musick shows ye have your closes,
And all must die.

Onely a sweet and vertuous soul,
Like season'd timber, never gives;
But though the whole world turn to coal,
Then chiefly lives.

THE PEARL

(Matthew xiii.)

I know the wayes of learning; both the head
And pipes that feed the presse, and make it runne;
What reason hath from nature borrowed,
Or of it self, like a good huswife, spunne
In laws and policie; what the starres conspire,
What willing nature speaks, what forc'd by fire;
Both th' old discoveries, and the new-found seas,
The stock and surplus, cause and historie:
All these stand open, or I have the keyes:
Yet I love thee.

THE PEARL

I know the wayes of honour, what maintains
The quick returns of courtesie and wit:
In vies of favours whether partie gains,
When glorie swells the heart, and moldeth it
To all expressions both of hand and eye,
Which on the world a true-love-knot may tie,
And bear the bundle, wheresoe're it goes:
How many drammes of spirit there must be
To sell my life unto my friends or foes:
Yet I love thee.

I know the wayes of pleasure, the sweet strains,
The lullings and the relishes of it;
The propositions of hot bloud and brains;
What mirth and musick mean; what love and wit
Have done these twentie hundred yeares, and more:
I know the projects of unbridled store:
My stuffe is flesh, not brasse; my senses live,
And grumble oft, that they have more in me
Then he that curbs them, being but one to five:
Yet I love thee.

I know all these, and have them in my hand:
Therefore not sealed, but with open eyes
I flie to thee, and fully understand
Both the main sale, and the commodities;
And at what rate and price I have thy love;
With all the circumstances that may move:
Yet through the labyrinths, not my groveling wit,
But thy silk twist let down from heav'n to me.
Did both conduct and teach me, how by it
To climbe to thee.

AFFLICTION

BROKEN in pieces all asunder,
Lord hunt me not,
A thing forgot,
Once a poore creature, now a wonder,
A wonder tortur'd in the space
Betwixt this world and that of grace.

My thoughts are all a case of knives,
Wounding my heart
With scatter'd smart,
As watring pots give flowers their lives.
Nothing their furie can controll,
While they do wound and prick my soul.

All my attendants are at strife,
Quitting their place
Unto my face:
Nothing performs the task of life:
The elements are let loose to fight,
And while I live, trie out their right.

Oh help, my God! let not their plot
Kill them and me,
And also thee,
Who art my life: dissolve the knot,
As the sunne scatters by his light
All the rebellions of the night.

Then shall those powers, which work for grief,
Enter thy pay,
And day by day
Labour thy praise, and my relief;
With care and courage building me,
Till I reach heav'n, and much more thee.

MAN

My God, I heard this day,
That none doth build a stately habitation,
But he that means to dwell therein.
What house more stately hath there been,
Or can be, then is Man? to whose creation
All things are in decay.

For Man is ev'ry thing,
And more: He is a tree, yet bears no fruit;
A beast, yet is, or should be more:
Reason and speech we onely bring.
Parrats may thank us, if they are not mute,
They go upon the score.

Man is all symmetrie,
Full of proportions, one limbe to another,
And all to all the world besides:
Each part may call the farthest, brother:
For head with foot hath private amitie,
And both with moons and tides.

Nothing hath got so farre,
But Man hath caught and kept it, as his prey.
His eyes dismount the highest starre:
He is in little all the sphere.
Herbs gladly cure our flesh; because that they
Finde their acquaintance there.

For us the windes do blow,
The earth doth rest, heav'n move, and fountains flow.
Nothing we see, but means our good,
As our *delight*, or as our *treasure:*
The whole is, either our cupboard of *food*,
Or cabinet of *pleasure*.

The starres have us to bed;
Night draws the curtain, which the sunne withdraws;
Musick and light attend our head.
All things unto our *flesh* are kinde
In their *descent* and *being;* to our *minde*
In their *ascent* and *cause*.

Each thing is full of dutie:
Waters united are our navigation;
Distinguished, our habitation;
Below, our drink; above, our meat;
Both are our cleanlinesse. Hath one such beautie?
Then how are all things neat?

More servants wait on Man,
Then he'l take notice of: in ev'ry path
He treads down that which doth befriend him,
When sicknesse makes him pale and wan.
Oh mightie love! Man is one world, and hath
Another to attend him

ANTIPHON

Since then, my God, thou hast
So brave a Palace built; O dwell in it,
That it may dwell with thee at last!
Till then, afford us so much wit;
That, as the world serves us, we may serve thee,
And both thy servants be.

ANTIPHON

Chor. PRAISED be the God of love,
Men. Here below,
Angels. And here above:
Cho. Who hath dealt his mercies so,
Ang. To his friend,
Men. And to his foe;

Cho. That both grace and glorie tend
Ang. Us of old,
Men. And us in th' end.
Cho. The great shepherd of the fold
Ang. Us did make,
Men. For us was sold.

Cho. He our foes in pieces brake;
Ang. Him we touch;
Men. And him we take.
Cho. Wherefore since that he is such,
Ang. We adore,
Men. And we do crouch.

Cho. Lord, thy praises should be more.
Men. We have none,
Ang. And we no store.
Cho. Praised be the God alone,
Who hath made of two folds one.

UNKINDNESSE

LORD, make me coy and tender to offend:
In friendship, first I think, if that agree,
Which I intend,
Unto my friends intent and end.
I would not use a friend, as I use Thee.

If any touch my friend, or his good name;
It is my honour and my love to free
His blasted fame
From the least spot or thought of blame.
I could not use a friend, as I use Thee.

My friend may spit upon my curious floore:
Would he have gold? I lend it instantly;
But let the poore,
And thou within them starve at doore.
I cannot use a friend, as I use Thee.

When that my friend pretendeth to a place,
I quit my interest, and leave it free:
But when thy grace
Sues for my heart, I thee displace,
Nor would I use a friend, as I use Thee.

Yet can a friend what thou hast done fulfill?
O write in brasse, *My God upon a tree*
His bloud did spill
Onely to purchase my good-will:
Yet use I not my foes, as I use thee.

LIFE

I MADE a posie, while the day ran by:
Here will I smell my remnant out, and tie
My life within this band.
But time did becken to the flowers, and they
By noon most cunningly did steal away,
And wither'd in my hand.

My hand was next to them, and then my heart:
I took, without more thinking, in good part
Times gentle admonition:
Who did so sweetly deaths sad taste convey,
Making my minde to smell my fatall day;
Yet sugring the suspicion.

Farewell deare flowers, sweetly your time ye spent,
Fit, while ye liv'd, for smell or ornament,
And after death for cures.
I follow straight without complaints or grief,
Since if my sent be good, I care not, if
It be as short as yours.

SUBMISSION

RR

But that thou art my wisdome, Lord,
  And both mine eyes are thine,
My minde would be extreamly stirr'd
  For missing my designe.

Were it not better to bestow
  Some place and power on me?
Then should thy praises with me grow,
  And share in my degree.

But when I thus dispute and grieve,
  I do resume my sight,
And pilfring what I once did give,
  Disseize thee of thy right.

How know I, if thou shouldst me raise,
  That I should then raise thee?
Perhaps great places and thy praise
  Do not so well agree.

Wherefore unto my gift I stand;
  I will no more advise:
Onely do thou lend me a hand,
  Since thou hast both mine eyes.

JUSTICE

I cannot skill of these thy wayes.
Lord, thou didst make me, yet thou woundest me;
Lord, thou dost wound me, yet thou dost relieve me:
Lord, thou relievest, yet I die by thee:
Lord, thou dost kill me, yet thou dost reprieve me.

But when I mark my life and praise,
Thy justice me most fitly payes:
For, *I do praise thee, yet I praise thee not:*
My prayers mean thee, yet my prayers stray:
I would do well, yet sinne the hand hath got:
My soul doth love thee, yet it loves delay.
I cannot skill of these my wayes.

CHARMS AND KNOTS

WHO reade a chapter when they rise,
Shall ne're be troubled with ill eyes.

A poore mans rod, when thou dost ride,
Is both a weapon and a guide.

Who shuts his hand, hath lost his gold:
Who opens it, hath it twice told.

Who goes to bed and doth not pray,
Maketh two nights to ev'ry day.

Who by aspersions throw a stone
At th' head of others, hit their own.

Who looks on ground with humble eyes,
Findes himself there, and seeks to rise.

When th' hair is sweet through pride or lust,
The powder doth forget the dust.

Take one from ten, and what remains?
Ten still, if sermons go for gains.

In shallow waters heav'n doth show;
But who drinks on, to hell may go.

AFFLICTION

My God, I read this day,
That planted Paradise was not so firm,
As was and is thy floting Ark ; whose stay
And anchor thou art onely, to confirm
And strengthen it in ev'ry age,
When waves do rise, and tempests rage.

At first we liv'd in pleasure ;
Thine own delights thou didst to us impart :
When we grew wanton, thou didst use displeasure
To make us thine : yet that we might not part,
As we at first did board with thee,
Now thou wouldst taste our miserie.

There is but joy and grief ;
If either will convert us, we are thine :
Some Angels us'd the first ; if our relief
Take up the second, then thy double line
And sev'rall baits in either kinde
Furnish thy table to thy minde.

Affliction then is ours ;
We are the trees, whom shaking fastens more,
While blustring windes destroy the wanton bowres,
And ruffle all their curious knots and store.
My God, so temper joy and wo,
That thy bright beams may tame thy bow.

MORTIFICATION

How soon doth man decay!
When clothes are taken from a chest of sweets
To swaddle infants, whose young breath
Scarce knows the way;
Those clouts are little winding sheets,
Which do consigne and send them unto death.

When boyes go first to bed,
They step into their voluntarie graves,
Sleep bindes them fast; onely their breath
Makes them not dead:
Successive nights, like rolling waves,
Convey them quickly, who are bound for death.

When youth is frank and free,
And calls for musick, while his veins do swell,
All day exchanging mirth and breath
In companie;
That musick summons to the knell,
Which shall befriend him at the house of death.

When man grows staid and wise,
Getting a house and home, where he may move
Within the circle of his breath,
Schooling his eyes;
That dumbe inclosure maketh love
Unto the coffin, that attends his death.

When age grows low and weak,
Marking his grave, and thawing ev'ry yeare,
Till all do melt, and drown his breath
When he would speak;
A chair or litter shows the biere,
Which shall convey him to the house of death.

Man, ere he is aware,
Hath put together a solemnitie,
And drest his herse, while he has breath
As yet to spare:
Yet Lord, instruct us so to die,
That all these dyings may be life in death.

DECAY

Sweet were the dayes, when thou didst lodge with
Struggle with Jacob, sit with Gideon, [Lot,
Advise with Abraham, when thy power could not
Encounter Moses strong complaints and mone:
Thy words were then, *Let me alone.*

One might have sought and found thee presently
At some fair oak, or bush, or cave, or well:
Is my God this way? No, they would reply:
He is to Sinai gone, as we heard tell:
List, ye may heare great Aarons bell.

But now thou dost thy self immure and close
In some one corner of a feeble heart:
Where yet both Sinne and Satan, thy old foes,
Do pinch and straiten thee, and use much art
To gain thy thirds and little part.

MISERIE

I see the world grows old, when as the heat
Of thy great love once spread, as in an urn
Doth closet up it self, and still retreat,
Cold sinne still forcing it, till it return,
        And calling Justice, all things burn.

MISERIE

Lord, let the Angels praise thy name.
Man is a foolish thing, a foolish thing,
Folly and Sinne play all his game.
His house still burns, and yet he still doth sing,
        Man is but grasse,
        He knows it, fill the glasse.

How canst thou brook his foolishnesse?
Why he'l not lose a cup of drink for thee:
Bid him but temper his excesse;
Not he: he knows, where he can better be,
        As he will swear,
        Then to serve thee in fear.

What strange pollutions doth he wed,
And make his own? as if none knew, but he.
No man shall beat into his head,
That thou within his curtains drawn canst see:
        They are of cloth,
        Where never yet came moth.

The best of men, turn but thy hand
For one poore minute, stumble at a pinne:
They would not have their actions scann'd,
Nor any sorrow tell them that they sinne,
Though it be small,
And measure not their fall.

They quarrell thee, and would give over
The bargain made to serve thee: but thy love
Holds them unto it, and doth cover
Their follies with the wing of thy milde Dove,
Not suff'ring those
Who would, to be thy foes.

My God, Man cannot praise thy name:
Thou art all brightnesse, perfect puritie;
The sunne holds down his head for shame,
Dead with eclipses, when we speak of thee:
How shall infection
Presume on thy perfection?

As dirtie hands foul all they touch,
And those things most, which are most pure and fine
So our clay hearts, ev'n when we crouch
To sing thy praises, make them lesse divine.
Yet either this,
Or none thy portion is.

Man cannot serve thee; let him go,
And serve the swine: there, there is his delight:
He doth not like this vertue, no;
Give him his dirt to wallow in all night:
These Preachers make
His head to shoot and ake.

MISERIE

Oh foolish man! where are thine eyes?
How hast thou lost them in a croud of cares?
Thou pull'st the rug, and wilt not rise,
No not to purchase the whole pack of starres:
There let them shine,
Thou must go sleep, or dine.

The bird that sees a daintie bowre
Made in the tree, where she was wont to sit,
Wonders and sings, but not his power
Who made the arbour: this exceeds her wit.
But Man doth know
The spring, whence all things flow:

And yet as though he knew it not,
His knowledge winks, and lets his humours reigne;
They make his life a constant blot,
And all the bloud of God to run in vain.
Ah wretch! what verse
Can thy strange wayes rehearse?

Indeed at first Man was a treasure,
A box of jewels, shop of rarities,
A ring, whose posie was, *My pleasure:*
He was a garden in a Paradise:
Glorie and grace
Did crown his heart and face.

But sinne hath fool'd him. Now he is
A lump of flesh, without a foot or wing
To raise him to the glimpse of blisse:
A sick toss'd vessel, dashing on each thing;
Nay, his own shelf:
My God, I mean my self.

JORDAN

WHEN first my lines of heav'nly joyes made mention,
Such was their lustre, they did so excell,
That I sought out quaint words, and trim invention;
My thoughts began to burnish, sprout, and swell,
Curling with metaphors a plain intention,
Decking the sense, as if it were to sell.

Thousands of notions in my brain did runne,
Off'ring their service, if I were not sped:
I often blotted what I had begunne;
This was not quick enough, and that was dead.
Nothing could seem too rich to clothe the sunne,
Much lesse those joyes which trample on his head.

As flames do work and winde, when they ascend,
So did I weave my self into the sense.
But while I bustled, I might heare a friend
Whisper, *How wide is all this long pretence!*
There is in love a sweetnesse readie penn'd:
Copie out onely that, and save expense.

PRAYER

OF what an easie quick accesse,
My blessed Lord, art thou! how suddenly
May our requests thine eare invade!
To shew that state dislikes not easinesse.
If I but lift mine eyes, my suit is made:
Thou canst no more not heare, then thou canst die.

Of what supreme almightie power
Is thy great arm which spans the east and west,
And tacks the centre to the sphere!
By it do all things live their measur'd houre:
We cannot ask the thing, which is not there,
Blaming the shallownesse of our request.

Of what unmeasurable love
Art thou possest, who, when thou couldst not die,
Wert fain to take our flesh and curse,
And for our sakes in person sinne reprove,
That by destroying that which ty'd thy purse,
Thou mightst make way for liberalitie!

Since then these three wait on thy throne,
Ease, *Power*, and *Love*; I value prayer so,
That were I to leave all but one,
Wealth, fame, endowments, vertues, all should go;
I and deare prayer would together dwell,
And quickly gain, for each inch lost, an ell.

OBEDIENCE

My God, if writings may
Convey a Lordship any way
Whither the buyer and the seller please;
Let it not thee displease,
If this poore paper do as much as they.

On it my heart doth bleed
As many lines, as there doth need
To passe it self and all it hath to thee,
To which I do agree,
And here present it as my speciall deed.

If that hereafter Pleasure
Cavill, and claim her part and measure,
As if this passed with a reservation,
Or some such words in fashion;
I here exclude the wrangler from thy treasure.

O let thy sacred will
All thy delight in me fulfill!
Let me not think an action mine own way,
But as thy love shall sway,
Resigning up the rudder to thy skill.

Lord, what is man to thee,
That thou shouldst mind a rotten tree?
Yet since thou canst not choose but see my actions
So great are thy perfections,
Thou mayst as well my actions guide, as see.

Besides, thy death and bloud
Show'd a strange love to all our good:
Thy sorrows were in earnest; no faint proffer,
Or superficiall offer
Of what we might not take, or be withstood.

Wherefore I all forgo:
To one word onely I say, No:
Where in the deed there was an intimation
Of a *gift* or *donation*,
Lord, let it now by way of *purchase* go.

He that will passe his land,
As I have mine, may set his hand
And heart unto this deed, when he hath read;
And make the purchase spread
To both our goods, if he to it will stand.

How happie were my part,
If some kinde man would thrust his heart
Into these lines; till in heav'ns court of rolls
They were by winged souls
Entred for both, farre above their desert!

CONSCIENCE

Peace pratler, do not lowre:
Not a fair look, but thou dost call it foul:
Not a sweet dish, but thou dost call it sowre:
Musick to thee doth howl.
By listning to thy chatting fears
I have both lost mine eyes and eares.

Pratler, no more, I say:
My thoughts must work, but like a noiseless sphere;
Harmonious peace must rock them all the day:
No room for pratlers there.
If thou persistest, I will tell thee,
That I have physick to expell thee.

And the receit shall be
My Saviours bloud: when ever at his board
I do but taste it, straight it cleanseth me,
And leaves thee not a word;
No, not a tooth or nail to scratch,
And at my actions carp, or catch.

Yet if thou talkest still,
Besides my physick, know there's some for thee:
Some wood and nails to make a staffe or bill
For those that trouble me:
The bloudie crosse of my deare Lord
Is both my physick and my sword.

SION

LORD, with what glorie wast thou serv'd of old,
When Solomons temple stood and flourished!
    Where most things were of purest gold;
    The wood was all embellished
With flowers and carvings, mysticall and rare:
All show'd the builders, crav'd the seers care.

Yet all this glorie, all this pomp and state
Did not affect thee much, was not thy aim;
    Something there was, that sow'd debate:
    Wherefore thou quitt'st thy ancient claim:
And now thy Architecture meets with sinne;
For all thy frame and fabrick is within.

There thou art struggling with a peevish heart,
Which sometimes crosseth thee, thou sometimes it:
    The fight is hard on either part.
    Great God doth fight, he doth submit.
All Solomons sea of brasse and world of stone
Is not so deare to thee as one good grone.

And truly brasse and stones are heavie things,
Tombes for the dead, not temples fit for thee:
    But grones are quick, and full of wings,
    And all their motions upward be;
And ever as they mount, like larks they sing;
The note is sad, yet musick for a king.

HOME

HOME

Come, Lord, my head doth burn, my heart is sick,
While thou dost ever, ever stay:
Thy long deferrings wound me to the quick,
My spirit gaspeth night and day.
O show thy self to me,
Or take me up to thee!

How canst thou stay, considering the pace
The bloud did make, which thou didst waste?
When I behold it trickling down thy face,
I never saw thing make such haste.
O show thy, &c.

When man was lost, thy pitie lookt about
To see what help in th' earth or skie:
But there was none; at least no help without:
The help did in thy bosome lie.
O show thy, &c.

There lay thy sonne: and must he leave that nest,
That hive of sweetnesse, to remove
Thraldome from those, who would not at a feast
Leave one poore apple for thy love?
O show thy, &c.

He did, he came: O my Redeemer deare,
After all this canst thou be strange?
So many yeares baptiz'd, and not appeare?
As if thy love could fail or change.
O show thy, &c.

Yet if thou stayest still, why must I stay?
My God, what is this world to me?
This world of wo? hence all ye clouds, away,
Away; I must get up and see.
O show thy self to me,
Or take me up to thee!

What is this weary world; this meat and drink,
That chains us by the teeth so fast?
What is this woman-kinde, which I can wink
Into a blacknesse and distaste?
O show thy, &c.

With one small sigh thou gav'st me th' other day
I blasted all the joyes about me:
And scouling on them as they pin'd away,
Now come again, said I, and flout me.
O show thy, &c.

Nothing but drought and dearth, but bush and brake,
Which way so-e're I look, I see.
Some may dream merrily, but when they wake,
They dresse themselves and come to thee.
O show thy, &c.

We talk of harvests; there are no such things,
But when we leave our corn and hay:
There is no fruitfull yeare, but that which brings
The last and lov'd, though dreadfull day.
O show thy, &c.

Oh loose this frame, this knot of man untie!
That my free soul may use her wing,
Which now is pinion'd with mortalitie,
As an intangled, hamper'd thing.
O show thy, &c.

What have I left, that I should stay and grone?
The most of me to heav'n is fled:
My thoughts and joyes are all packt up and gone,
And for their old acquaintance plead.
O show thy self to me,
Or take me up to thee!

Come dearest Lord, pass not this holy season,
My flesh and bones and joynts do pray:
And ev'n my verse, when by the ryme and reason
The word is, *Stay*, sayes ever, *Come*.
O show thy, &c.

THE BRITISH CHURCH

I JOY, deare Mother, when I view
Thy perfect lineaments, and hue
Both sweet and bright.

Beautie in thee takes up her place,
And dates her letters from thy face,
When she doth write.

A fine aspect in fit aray,
Neither too mean, nor yet too gay,
Shows who is best.

Outlandish looks may not compare:
For all they either painted are,
Or else undrest.

She on the hills, which wantonly
Allureth all, in hope to be
By her preferr'd,

Hath kiss'd so long her painted shrines,
That ev'n her face by kissing shines,
For her reward.

She in the valley is so shie
Of dressing, that her hair doth lie
About her eares:

While she avoids her neighbours pride,
She wholly goes on th' other side,
And nothing wears.

But dearest Mother, (what those misse)
The mean thy praise and glorie is,
And long may be.

Blessed be God, whose love it was
To double-moat thee with his grace,
And none but thee.

THE QUIP

The merrie world did on a day
With his train-bands and mates agree
To meet together, where I lay,
And all in sport to geere at me.

First, Beautie crept into a rose,
Which when I pluckt not, Sir, said she,
Tell me, I pray, Whose hands are those?
But thou shalt answer, Lord, for me.

Then Money came, and chinking still,
What tune is this, poore man? said he:
I heard in Musick you had skill.
But thou shalt answer, Lord, for me.

Then came brave Glorie puffing by
In silks that whistled, who but he?
He scarce allow'd me half an eie.
But thou shalt answer, Lord, for me.

Then came quick Wit and Conversation,
And he would needs a comfort be,
And, to be short, make an oration.
But thou shalt answer, Lord, for me.

Yet when the houre of thy designe
To answer these fine things shall come;
Speak not at large, say, I am thine:
And then they have their answer home.

VANITIE

Poore silly soul, whose hope and head lies low;
Whose flat delights on earth do creep and grow;
To whom the starres shine not so fair, as eyes;
Nor solid work, as false embroyderies;
Heark and beware, lest what you now do measure
And write for sweet, prove a most sowre displeasure

O heare betimes, lest thy relenting
May come too late!
To purchase heaven for repenting,
Is no hard rate.

If souls be made of earthly mold,
Let them love gold;
If born on high,
Let them unto their kindred flie:
For they can never be at rest,
Till they regain their ancient nest.
Then silly soul take heed; for earthly joy
Is but a bubble, and makes thee a boy.

THE DAWNING

Awake sad heart, whom sorrow ever drowns;
Take up thine eyes, which feed on earth;
Unfold thy forehead gather'd into frowns:
Thy Saviour comes, and with him mirth:
Awake, awake;
And with a thankfull heart his comforts take.
But thou dost still lament, and pine, and crie;
And feel his death, but not his victorie.

Arise sad heart; if thou dost not withstand,
Christs resurrection thine may be:
Do not by hanging down break from the hand,
Which as it riseth, raiseth thee:
Arise, arise;
And with his buriall-linen drie thine eyes:
Christ left his grave-clothes, that we might, when grief
Draws tears, or bloud, not want an handkerchief.

JESU

JESU is in my heart, his sacred name
Is deeply carved there: but th'other week
A great affliction broke the little frame,
Ev'n all to pieces: which I went to seek:
And first I found the corner, where was *J*,
After, where *E S*, and next where *U* was graved.
When I had got these parcels, instantly
I sat me down to spell them, and perceived
That to my broken heart he was *I ease you*,
And to my whole is *JESU*.

BUSINESSE

CANST be idle? canst thou play,
Foolish soul who sinn'd to-day?

Rivers run, and springs each one
Know their home, and get them gone:
Hast thou tears, or hast thou none?

If, poore soul, thou hast no tears;
Would thou hadst no faults or fears!
Who hath these, those ill forbears.

Windes still work: it is their plot,
Be the season cold, or hot:
Hast thou sighs, or hast thou not?

If thou hast no sighs or grones,
Would thou hadst no flesh and bones!
Lesser pains scape greater ones.

But if yet thou idle be,
Foolish soul, Who di'd for thee?

Who did leave his Fathers throne,
To assume thy flesh and bone;
Had he life, or had he none?

If he had not liv'd for thee,
Thou hadst di'd most wretchedly;
And two deaths had been thy fee.

He so farre thy good did plot,
That his own self he forgot.
Did he die, or did he not?

If he had not di'd for thee,
Thou hadst liv'd in miserie.
Two lives worse then ten deaths be.

And hath any space of breath
'Twixt his sinnes and Saviours death?

He that loseth gold, though drosse,
Tells to all he meets, his crosse:
He that sinnes, hath he no losse?

He that findes a silver vein,
Thinks on it, and thinks again:
Brings thy Saviours death no gain?

Who in heart not ever kneels,
Neither sinne nor Saviour feels.

DIALOGUE

SWEETEST Saviour, if my soul
Were but worth the having,
Quickly should I then controll
Any thought of waving.
But when all my care and pains
Cannot give the name of gains
To thy wretch so full of stains;
What delight or hope remains?

What (childe) is the ballance thine,
Thine the poise and measure?
If I say, Thou shalt be mine;
Finger not my treasure.
What the gains in having thee
Do amount to, onely he,
Who for man was sold, can see;
That transferr'd th' accounts to me.

But as I can see no merit,
Leading to this favour:
So the way to fit me for it,
Is beyond my savour.
As the reason then is thine;
So the way is none of mine:
I disclaim the whole designe:
Sinne disclaims and I resigne.

That is all, if that I could
Get without repining;
And my clay my creature would
Follow my resigning.

That as I did freely part
With my glorie and desert,
Left all joyes to feel all smart—
Ah! no more: thou break'st my heart.

DULNESSE

Why do I languish thus, drooping and dull,
As if I were all earth?
O give me quicknesse, that I may with mirth
Praise thee brim-full!

The wanton lover in a curious strain
Can praise his fairest fair;
And with quaint metaphors her curled hair
Curl o're again.

Thou art my lovelinesse, my life, my light,
Beautie alone to me:
Thy bloudy death and undeserv'd, makes thee
Pure red and white.

When all perfections as but one appeare,
That those thy form doth show,
The very dust, where thou dost tread and go,
Makes beauties here;

Where are my lines then? my approaches? views?
Where are my window-songs?
Lovers are still pretending, & ev'n wrongs
Sharpen their Muse:

But I am lost in flesh, whose sugred lyes
Still mock me, and grow bold:
Sure thou didst put a minde there, if I could
Finde where it lies.

Lord, cleare thy gift, that with a constant wit
I may but look towards thee:
Look onely; for to *love* thee, who can be,
What angel fit?

LOVE-JOY

As on a window late I cast mine eye,
I saw a vine drop grapes with *J* and *C*
Anneal'd on every bunch. One standing by
Ask'd what it meant. I (who am never loth
To spend my iudgement) said, It seem'd to me
To be the bodie and the letters both
Of *Joy* and *Charitie*. Sir, you have not miss'd,
The man reply'd; It figures *JESUS CHRIST*.

PROVIDENCE

O Sacred Providence, who from end to end
Strongly and sweetly movest! shall I write,
And not of thee, through whom my fingers bend
To hold my quill? shall they not do thee right?

Of all the creatures both in sea and land
Onely to Man thou hast made known thy wayes,
And put the penne alone into his hand,
And made him Secretarie of thy praise.

Beasts fain would sing; birds dittie to their notes;
Trees would be tuning on their native lute
To thy renown: but all their hands and throats
Are brought to Man, while they are lame and mute.

Man is the worlds high Priest: he doth present
The sacrifice for all; while they below
Unto the service mutter an assent,
Such as springs use that fall, and windes that blow.

He that to praise and laud thee doth refrain,
Doth not refrain unto himself alone,
But robs a thousand who would praise thee fain,
And doth commit a world of sinne in one.

The beasts say, Eat me: but, if beasts must teach,
The tongue is yours to eat, but mine to praise.
The trees say, Pull me: but the hand you stretch,
Is mine to write, as it is yours to raise.

Wherefore, most sacred Spirit, I here present
For me and all my fellows praise to thee:
And just it is that I should pay the rent,
Because the benefit accrues to me.

We all acknowledge both thy power and love
To be exact, transcendent, and divine;
Who dost so strongly and so sweetly move,
While all things have their will, yet none but thine.

For either thy *command*, or thy *permission*
Lay hands on all: they are thy *right* and *left*.
The first puts on with speed and expedition;
The other curbs sinnes stealing pace and theft.

Nothing escapes them both; all must appeare,
And be dispos'd, and dress'd, and tun'd by thee,
Who sweetly temper'st all. If we could heare
Thy skill and art, what musick would it be!

Thou art in small things great, not small in any:
Thy even praise can neither rise, nor fall.
Thou art in all things one, in each thing many:
For thou art infinite in one and all.

Tempests are calm to thee; they know thy hand,
And hold it fast, as children do their fathers,
Which crie and follow. Thou hast made poore sand
Check the proud sea, ev'n when it swells and gathers.

Thy cupboard serves the world: the meat is set,
Where all may reach: no beast but knows his feed.
Birds teach us hawking; fishes have their net:
The great prey on the lesse, they on some weed.

Nothing ingendred doth prevent his meat:
Flies have their table spread, ere they appeare.
Some creatures have in winter what to eat;
Others do sleep, and envie not their cheer.

How finely dost thou times and seasons spin,
And make a twist checker'd with night and day!
Which as it lengthens windes, and windes us in,
As bouls go on, but turning all the way.

Each creature hath a wisdome for his good.
The pigeons feed their tender off-spring, crying,
When they are callow; but withdraw their food
When they are fledge, that need may teach thẽ flying.

Bees work for man; and yet they never bruise
Their masters flower, but leave it, having done,
As fair as ever, and as fit to use;
So both the flower doth stay, and hony run.

Sheep eat the grasse, and dung the ground for more:
Trees after bearing drop their leaves for soil:
Springs vent their streams, and by expense get store:
Clouds cool by heat, and baths by cooling boil.

Who hath the vertue to expresse the rare
And curious vertues both of herbs and stones?
Is there an herb for that? O that thy care
Would show a root, that gives expressions!

And if an herb hath power, what have the starres?
A rose, besides his beautie, is a cure.
Doubtlesse our plagues and plentie, peace and warres
Are there much surer then our art is sure.

Thou hast hid metals: man may take them thence;
But at his peril: when he digs the place,
He makes a grave; as if the thing had sense,
And threatned man, that he should fill the space.

Ev'n poysons praise thee. Should a thing be lost?
Should creatures want for want of heed their due?
Since where are poysons, antidots are most:
The help stands close, and keeps the fear in view.

The sea, which seems to stop the traveller,
Is by a ship the speedier passage made.
The windes, who think they rule the mariner,
Are rul'd by him, and taught to serve his trade.

And as thy house is full, so I adore
Thy curious art in marshalling thy goods.
The hills with health abound; the vales with store;
The South with marble; North with furres & woods.

Hard things are glorious; easie things good cheap.
The common all men have; that which is rare,
Men therefore seek to have, and care to keep.
The healthy frosts with summer-fruits compare.

Light without winde is glasse: warm without weight
Is wooll and furres: cool without closenesse, shade:
Speed without pains, a horse: tall without height,
A servile hawk: low without losse, a spade.

All countreys have enough to serve their need:
If they seek fine things, thou dost make them run
For their offence; and then dost turn their speed
To be commerce and trade from sunne to sunne.

Nothing wears clothes, but Man; nothing doth need
But he to wear them. Nothing useth fire,
But Man alone, to show his heav'nly breed:
And onely he hath fuell in desire.

When th' earth was dry, thou mad'st a sea of wet:
Whẽ that lay gather'd, thou didst broach the moũtains:
When yet some places could no moisture get, [tains.
The windes grew gard'ners, and the clouds good foun-

Rain, do not hurt my flowers; but gently spend
Your hony drops: presse not to smell them here:
When they are ripe, their odour will ascend,
And at your lodging with their thanks appeare.

How harsh are thorns to pears! and yet they make
A better hedge, and need lesse reparation.
How smooth are silks compared with a stake,
Or with a stone! yet make no good foundation.

Sometimes thou dost divide thy gifts to man,
Sometimes unite. The Indian nut alone
Is clothing, meat and trencher, drink and kan,
Boat, cable, sail and needle, all in one.

Most herbs that grow in brooks, are hot and dry.
Cold fruits warm kernells help against the winde.
The lemmons juice and rinde cure mutually.
The whey of milk doth loose, the milk doth binde.

Thy creatures leap not, but expresse a feast,
Where all the guests sit close, and nothing wants.
Frogs marry fish and flesh; bats, bird and beast;
Sponges, non-sense and sense; mines, th' earth & plants.

To show thou art not bound, as if thy lot
Were worse then ours; sometimes thou shiftest hands.
Most things move th' under-jaw; the Crocodile not.
Most things sleep lying; th' Elephant leans or stands.

But who hath praise enough? nay who hath any?
None can expresse thy works, but he that knows them:
And none can know thy works, which are so many,
And so complete, but onely he that owes them.

All things that are, though they have sev'rall wayes,
Yet in their being joyn with one advise
To honour thee: and so I give thee praise
In all my other hymnes, but in this twice.

Each thing that is, although in use and name
It go for one, hath many wayes in store
To honour thee ; and so each hymne thy fame
Extolleth many wayes, yet this one more.

HOPE

I GAVE to Hope a watch of mine : but he
An anchor gave to me.
Then an old prayer-book I did present :
And he an optick sent.
With that I gave a viall full of tears :
But he a few green eares :
Ah Loyterer ! I'le no more, no more I'le bring :
I did expect a ring.

SINNES ROUND

SORRIE I am, my God, sorrie I am,
That my offences course it in a ring.
My thoughts are working like a busie flame,
Untill their cockatrice they hatch and bring :
And when they once have perfected their draughts,
My words take fire from my inflamed thoughts.

My words take fire from my inflamed thoughts,
Which spit it forth like the Sicilian hill.
They vent the wares, and passe them with their faults,
And by their breathing ventilate the ill.
But words suffice not, where are lewd intentions :
My hands do joyn to finish the inventions.

My hands do joyn to finish the inventions:
And so my sinnes ascend three stories high,
As Babel grew, before there were dissentions.
Yet ill deeds loyter not: for they supplie
New thoughts of sinning: wherefore, to my shame,
Sorrie I am, my God, sorrie I am.

TIME

Meeting with Time, slack thing, said I,
Thy sithe is dull; whet it for shame.
No marvell Sir, he did replie,
If it at length deserve some blame:
 But where one man would have me grinde it,
 Twentie for one too sharp do finde it.

Perhaps some such of old did passe,
Who above all things lov'd this life;
To whom thy sithe a hatchet was,
Which now is but a pruning-knife.
 Christs coming hath made man thy debter,
 Since by thy cutting he grows better.

And in his blessing thou art blest:
For where thou onely wert before
An executioner at best;
Thou art a gard'ner now, and more,
 An usher to convey our souls
 Beyond the utmost starres and poles.

And this is that makes life so long,
While it detains us from our God.
Ev'n pleasures here increase the wrong,
And length of dayes lengthen the rod.
  Who wants the place, where God doth dwell,
  Partakes already half of hell.

Of what strange length must that needs be,
Which ev'n eternitie excludes!
Thus farre Time heard me patiently:
Then chafing said, This man deludes:
  What do I here before his doore?
  He doth not crave lesse time, but more.

GRATEFULNESSE

THOU that hast giv'n so much to me,
Give one thing more, a gratefull heart.
See how thy beggar works on thee
By art.

He makes thy gifts occasion more,
And sayes, If he in this be crost,
All thou hast giv'n him heretofore
Is lost.

But thou didst reckon, when at first
Thy word our hearts and hands did crave,
What it would come to at the worst
To save.

Perpetuall knockings at thy doore,
Tears sullying thy transparent rooms,
Gift upon gift, much would have more,
And comes.

This not withstanding, thou wentst on,
And didst allow us all our noise:
Nay thou hast made a sigh and grone
Thy joyes.

Not that thou hast not still above
Much better tunes, then grones can make;
But that these countrey-aires thy love
Did take.

Wherefore I crie, and crie again;
And in no quiet canst thou be,
Till I a thankfull heart obtain
Of thee:

Not thankfull, when it pleaseth me;
As if thy blessings had spare dayes:
But such a heart, whose pulse may be
Thy praise.

PEACE

Sweet Peace, where dost thou dwell? I humbly crave,
Let me once know.
I sought thee in a secret cave,
And ask'd, if Peace were there.
A hollow winde did seem to answer, No:
Go seek elsewhere.

PEACE

I did; and going did a rainbow note:
Surely, thought I,
This is the lace of Peaces coat:
I will search out the matter.
But while I lookt, the clouds immediately
Did break and scatter.

Then went I to a garden, and did spy
A gallant flower,
The crown Imperiall: Sure, said I,
Peace at the root must dwell.
But when I digg'd, I saw a worm devoure
What show'd so well.

At length I met a rev'rend good old man,
Whom when for Peace
I did demand; he thus began:
There was a Prince of old
At Salem dwelt, who liv'd with good increase
Of flock and fold.

He sweetly liv'd; yet sweetnesse did not save
His life from foes.
But after death out of his grave
There sprang twelve stalks of wheat:
Which many wondring at, got some of those
To plant and set.

It prosper'd strangely, and did soon disperse
Through all the earth:
For they that taste it do rehearse,
That vertue lies therein,
A secret vertue bringing peace and mirth
By flight of sinne.

Take of this grain, which in my garden grows,
And grows for you;
Make bread of it: and that repose
And peace which ev'ry where
With so much earnestnesse you do pursue,
Is onely there.

CONFESSION

O WHAT a cunning guest
Is this same grief! within my heart I made
Closets; and in them many a chest;
And like a master in my trade,
In those chests, boxes; in each box, a till:
Yet grief knows all, and enters when he will.

No scrue, no piercer can
Into a piece of timber work and winde,
As Gods afflictions into man,
When he a torture hath design'd.
They are too subtill for the subt'llest hearts;
And fall, like rheumes, upon the tendrest parts.

We are the earth; and they,
Like moles within us, heave, and cast about:
And till they foot and clutch their prey,
They never cool, much lesse give out.
No smith can make such locks, but they have keyes:
Closets are halls to them; and hearts, high-wayes.

Onely an open breast
Doth shut them out, so that they cannot enter ;
Or, if they enter, cannot rest,
But quickly seek some new adventure.
Smooth open hearts no fastning have ; but fiction
Doth give a hold and handle to affliction.

Wherefore my faults and sinnes,
Lord, I acknowledge ; take thy plagues away :
For since confession pardon winnes,
I challenge here the brightest day,
The clearest diamond : let them do their best,
They shall be thick and cloudie to my breast.

GIDDINESSE

OH, what a thing is man ! how farre from power,
From setled peace and rest !
He is some twentie sev'rall men at least
Each sev'rall houre.

One while he counts of heav'n, as of his treasure :
But then a thought creeps in,
And calls him coward, who for fear of sinne
Will lose a pleasure.

Now he will fight it out, and to the warres ;
Now eat his bread in peace,
And snudge in quiet : now he scorns increase ;
Now all day spares.

He builds a house, which quickly down must go,
As if a whirlwinde blew
And crusht the building: and it's partly true,
His minde is so.

O what a sight were Man, if his attires
Did alter with his minde;
And like a Dolphins skinne, his clothes combin'd
With his desires!

Surely if each one saw anothers heart,
There would be no commerce,
No sale or bargain passe: all would disperse,
And live apart.

Lord, mend or rather make us: one creation
Will not suffice our turn:
Except thou make us dayly, we shall spurn
Our own salvation.

THE BUNCH OF GRAPES

Joy, I did lock thee up: but some bad man
Hath let thee out again:
And now, me thinks, I am where I began
Sev'n yeares ago: one vogue and vein,
One aire of thoughts usurps my brain.
I did toward Canaan draw; but now I am
Brought back to the Red sea, the sea of shame.

For as the Jews of old by Gods command
Travell'd, and saw no town:
So now each Christian hath his journeys spann'd:
Their storie pennes and sets us down.
A single deed is small renown.
Gods works are wide, and let in future times;
His ancient justice overflows our crimes.

Then have we too our guardian fires and clouds;
Our Scripture-dew drops fast:
We have our sands and serpents, tents and shrowds;
Alas! our murmurings come not last.
But where's the cluster? where's the taste
Of mine inheritance? Lord, if I must borrow,
Let me as well take up their joy, as sorrow.

But can he want the grape, who hath the wine?
I have their fruit and more.
Blessed be God, who prosper'd *Noahs* vine,
And made it bring forth grapes good store.
But much more him I must adore,
Who of the laws sowre juice sweet wine did make,
Ev'n God himself, being pressed for my sake.

LOVE UNKNOWN

DEARE Friend, sit down, the tale is long and sad:
And in my faintings I presume your loue
Will more complie, then help. A Lord I had,
And have, of whom some grounds which may improve,
I hold for two lives, and both lives in me.

To him I brought a dish of fruit one day,
And in the middle plac'd my heart. But he
(I sigh to say)
Lookt on a seruant, who did know his eye
Better then you know me, or (which is one)
Then I my self. The servant instantly
Quitting the fruit, seiz'd on my heart alone,
And threw it in a font, wherein did fall
A stream of bloud, which issu'd from the side
Of a great rock : I well remember all,
And have good cause : there it was dipt and di'd,
And washt, and wrung : the very wringing yet
Enforceth tears. *Your heart was foul, I fear.*
Indeed 'tis true. I did and do commit
Many a fault more then my lease will bear ;
Yet still askt pardon, and was not deni'd.
But you shall heare. After my heart was well,
And clean and fair, as I one even-tide
(I sigh to tell)
Walkt by my self abroad, I saw a large
And spacious fornace flaming, and thereon
A boyling caldron, round about whose verge
Was in great letters set *AFFLICTION*.
The greatnesse shew'd the owner. So I went
To fetch a sacrifice out of my fold,
Thinking with that, which I did thus present,
To warm his love, which I did fear grew cold.
But as my heart did tender it, the man
Who was to take it from me, slipt his hand,
And threw my heart into the scalding pan ;
My heart, that brought it (do you understand ?)
The offerers heart. *Your heart was hard, I fear.*
Indeed 'tis true. I found a callous matter
Began to spread and to expatiate there :

But with a richer drug, then scalding water,
I bath'd it often, ev'n with holy bloud,
Which at a board, while many drunk bare wine,
A friend did steal into my cup for good,
Ev'n taken inwardly, and most divine
To supple hardnesses. But at the length
Out of the caldron getting, soon I fled
Unto my house, where to repair the strength
Which I had lost, I hasted to my bed.
But when I thought to sleep out all these faults
(I sigh to speak)
I found that some had stuff'd the bed with thoughts,
I would say *thorns*. Deare, could my heart not break,
When with my pleasures ev'n my rest was gone?
Full well I understood, who had been there:
For I had giv'n the key to none, but one:
It must be he. *Your heart was dull, I fear.*
Indeed a slack and sleepie state of minde
Did oft possesse me, so that when I pray'd,
Though my lips went, my heart did stay behinde.
But all my scores were by another paid,
Who took the debt upon him. *Truly, Friend,*
For ought I heare, your Master shows to you
More favour then you wot of. Mark the end.
The Font did onely, what was old, renew:
The Caldron suppled, what was grown too hard:
The Thorns did quicken, what was grown too dull:
All did but strive to mend, what you had marr'd.
Wherefore be cheer'd, and praise him to the full
Each day, each houre, each moment of the week,
Who fain would have you be, new, tender, quick.

MANS MEDLEY

HEARK, how the birds do sing,
And woods do ring.
All creatures have their joy: and man hath his.
Yet if we rightly measure,
Mans joy and pleasure
Rather hereafter, then in present, is.

To this life things of sense
Make their pretence:
In th'other Angels have a right by birth:
Man ties them both alone,
And makes them one,
With th'one hand touching heav'n, with th'other earth.

In soul he mounts and flies,
In flesh he dies.
He wears a stuffe whose thread is course and round,
But trimm'd with curious lace,
And should take place
After the trimming, not the stuffe and ground.

Not, that he may not here
Taste of the cheer,
But as birds drink, and straight lift up their head,
So must he sip and think
Of better drink
He may attain to, after he is dead.

But as his joyes are double;
So is his trouble.
He hath two winters, other things but one:
Both frosts and thoughts do nip,
And bite his lip;
And he of all things fears two deaths alone.

Yet ev'n the greatest griefs
May be reliefs,
Could he but take them right, and in their wayes.
Happie is he, whose heart
Hath found the art
To turn his double pains to double praise.

THE STORM

If as the windes and waters here below
Do flie and flow,
My sighs and tears as busie were above;
Sure they would move
And much affect thee, as tempestuous times
Amaze poore mortals, and object their crimes.

Starres have their storms, ev'n in a high degree,
As well as we.
A throbbing conscience spurred by remorse
Hath a strange force:
It quits the earth, and mounting more and more,
Dares to assault thee, and besiege thy doore.

There it stands knocking, to thy musicks wrong,
And drowns the song.
Glorie and honour are set by till it
An answer get.
Poets have wrong'd poore storms: such dayes are best;
They purge the aire without, within the breast.

PARADISE

I BLESSE thee, Lord, because I GROW
Among thy trees, which in a ROW
To thee both fruit and order OW.

What open force, or hidden CHARM
Can blast my fruit, or bring me HARM,
While the inclosure is thine ARM?

Inclose me still for fear I START.
Be to me rather sharp and TART,
Then let me want thy hand & ART.

When thou dost greater judgements SPARE,
And with thy knife but prune and PARE,
Ev'n fruitfull trees more fruitfull ARE.

Such sharpnes shows the sweetest FREND:
Such cuttings rather heal then REND:
And such beginnings touch their END.

THE METHOD

Poore heart, lament.
For since thy God refuseth still,
There is some rub, some discontent,
Which cools his will.

Thy Father *could*
Quickly effect, what thou dost move;
For he is *Power:* and sure he *would;*
For he is *Love.*

Go search this thing,
Tumble thy breast, and turn thy book.
If thou hadst lost a glove or ring,
Wouldst thou not look?

What do I see
Written above there! *Yesterday*
I did behave me carelesly,
When I did pray.

And should Gods eare
To such indifferents chained be,
Who do not their own motions heare?
Is God lesse free?

But stay! what's there?
Late when I would have something done,
I had a motion to forbear,
Yet I went on.

And should God's eare,
Which needs not man, be ty'd to those
Who heare not him, but quickly heare
His utter foes?

Then once more pray:
Down with thy knees, up with thy voice.
Seek pardon first, and God will say,
Glad heart rejoyce.

DIVINITIE

As men, for fear the starres should sleep and nod,
And trip at night, have spheres suppli'd;
As if a starre were duller then a clod,
Which knows his way without a guide:

Just so the other heav'n they also serve,
Divinities transcendent skie:
Which with the edge of wit they cut and carve.
Reason triumphs, and faith lies by.

Could not that wisdome, which first broacht the wine,
Have thicken'd it with definitions?
And jagg'd his seamlesse coat, had that been fine,
With curious questions and divisions?

But all the doctrine, which he taught and gave,
Was cleare as heav'n, from whence it came.
At least those beams of truth, which onely save,
Surpasse in brightnesse any flame.

Love God, and love your neighbour. Watch and pray.
Do as ye would be done unto.
O dark instructions; ev'n as dark as day!
Who can these Gordian knots undo?

But he doth bid us take his bloud for wine.
Bid what he please; yet I am sure,
To take and taste what he doth there designe,
Is all that saves, and not obscure.

Then burn thy Epicycles, foolish man;
Break all thy spheres, and save thy head.
Faith needs no staffe of flesh, but stoutly can
To heav'n alone both go, and leade.

EPHES. 4. 30

Grieve not the Holy Spirit, &c.

And art thou grieved, sweet and sacred Dove,
When I am sowre,
And crosse thy love?
Grieved for me? the God of strength and power
Griev'd for a worm, which when I tread,
I passe away and leave it dead?

Then weep mine eyes, the God of love doth grieve
Weep foolish heart,
And weeping live:
For death is drie as dust. Yet if ye part,
End as the night, whose sable hue
Your sinnes expresse; melt into dew

When sawcie mirth shall knock or call at doore,
Cry out, Get hence,
Or cry no more.
Almightie God doth grieve, he puts on sense:
I sinne not to my grief alone,
But to my Gods too; he doth grone.

Oh take thy lute, and tune it to a strain,
Which may with thee
All day complain.
There can no discord but in ceasing be.
Marbles can weep; and surely strings
More bowels have, then such hard things.

Lord, I adjudge my self to tears and grief,
Ev'n endlesse tears
Without relief.
If a cleare spring for me no time forbears,
But runnes, although I be not drie;
I am no Crystall, what shall I?

Yet if I wail not still, since still to wail
Nature denies;
And flesh would fail,
If my deserts were masters of mine eyes:
Lord, pardon, for thy sonne makes good
My want of tears with store of bloud.

THE FAMILIE

What doth this noise of thoughts within my heart
As if they had a part?
What do these loud complaints and pulling fears,
As if there were no rule or eares?

But, Lord, the house and familie are thine,
Though some of them repine.
Turn out these wranglers, which defile thy seat:
For where thou dwellest all is neat.

First Peace and Silence all disputes controll,
Then Order plaies the soul;
And giving all things their set forms and houres,
Makes of wilde woods sweet walks and bowres.

Humble Obedience neare the doore doth stand,
Expecting a command:
Then whom in waiting nothing seems more slow,
Nothing more quick when she doth go.

Joyes oft are there, and griefs as oft as joyes;
But griefs without a noise:
Yet speak they louder, then distemper'd fears.
What is so shrill as silent tears?

This is thy house, with these it doth abound:
And where these are not found,
Perhaps thou com'st sometimes, and for a day;
But not to make a constant stay.

THE SIZE

Content thee, greedie heart.
Modest and moderate joyes to those, that have
Title to more hereafter when they part,
Are passing brave.
Let th' upper springs into the low
Descend and fall, and thou dost flow.

What though some have a fraught
Of cloves and nutmegs, and in cinamon sail;
If thou hast wherewithall to spice a draught,
When griefs prevail;
And for the future time art heir
To th' Isle of spices? Is't not fair?

To be in both worlds full
Is more then God was, who was hungrie here.
Wouldst thou his laws of fasting disanull?
Enact good cheer?
Lay out thy joy, yet hope to save it?
Wouldst thou both eat thy cake, and have it?

Great joyes are all at once;
But little do reserve themselves for more: [nounce,
Those have their hopes; these what they have re-
And live on score:
Those are at home; these journey still,
And meet the rest on Sions hill.

Thy Saviour sentenc'd joy,
And in the flesh condemn'd it as unfit,
At least in lump: for such doth oft destroy;
Whereas a bit
Doth tice us on to hopes of more,
And for the present health restore.

A Christians state and case
Is not a corpulent, but a thinne and spare,
Yet active strength: whose long and bonie face
Content and care
Do seem to equally divide,
Like a pretender, not a bride.

Wherefore sit down, good heart;
Grasp not at much, for fear thou losest all.
If comforts fell according to desert,
They would great frosts and snows destroy:
For we should count, Since the last joy.

Then close again the seam,
Which thou hast open'd: do not spread thy robe
In hope of great things. Call to minde thy dream,
An earthly globe,
On whose meridian was engraven,
These seas are tears, and heav'n the haven.

ARTILLERIE

As I one ev'ning sat before my cell,
Me thoughts a starre did shoot into my lap.
I rose, and shook my clothes, as knowing well,
That from small fires comes oft not small mishap.
When suddenly I heard one say,
Do as thou usest, disobey,
Expell good motions from thy breast,
Which have the face of fire, but end in rest.

I, who had heard of musick in the spheres,
But not of speech in starres, began to muse:
But turning to my God, whose ministers
The starres and all things are; If I refuse,
Dread Lord, said I, so oft my good;
Then I refuse not ev'n with bloud
To wash away my stubborn thought:
For I will do, or suffer what I ought.

But I have also starres and shooters too,
Born where thy servants both artilleries use.
My tears and prayers night and day do wooe,
And work up to thee; yet thou dost refuse.
Not, but I am (I must say still)
Much more oblig'd to do thy will,
Then thou to grant mine: but because
Thy promise now hath ev'n set thee thy laws.

Then we are shooters both, and thou dost deigne
To enter combate with us, and contest
With thine own clay. But I would parley fain:
Shunne not my arrows, and behold my breast.
Yet if thou shunnest, I am thine:
I must be so, if I am mine.
There is no articling with thee:
I am but finite, yet thine infinitely.

CHURCH-RENTS AND SCHISMES

Brave rose, (alas!) where art thou? in the chair
Where thou didst lately so triumph and shine,
A worm doth sit, whose many feet and hair
Are the more foul, the more thou wert divine.
This, this hath done it, this did bite the root
And bottome of the leaves: which when the winde
Did once perceive, it blew them under foot,
Where rude unhallow'd steps do crush and grinde
Their beauteous glories. Onely shreds of thee,
And those all bitten, in thy chair I see.

JUSTICE

Why doth my Mother blush ? is she the rose,
And shows it so ? Indeed Christs precious bloud
Gave you a colour once ; which when your foes
Thought to let out, the bleeding did you good,
And made you look much fresher then before.
But when debates and fretting jealousies
Did worm and work within you more and more,
Your colour faded, and calamities
    Turned your ruddie into pale and bleak :
    Your health and beautie both began to break.

Then did your sev'rall parts unloose and start :
Which when your neighbours saw, like a north-winde,
They rushed in, and cast them in the dirt
Where Pagans tread. O Mother deare and kinde,
Where shall I get me eyes enough to weep,
As many eyes as starres ? since it is night,
And much of Asia and Europe fast asleep,
And ev'n all Africk ; would at least I might
    With these two poore ones lick up all the dew,
    Which falls by night, and poure it out for you !

JUSTICE

O DREADFULL Justice, what a fright and terrour
                Wast thou of old,
                When sinne and errour
        Did show and shape thy looks to me,
        And through their glasse discolour thee !
He that did but look up, was proud and bold.

The dishes of thy ballance seem'd to gape,
Like two great pits;
The beam and scape
Did like some tort'ring engine show:
Thy hand above did burn and glow,
Danting the stoutest hearts, the proudest wits.

But now that Christs pure vail presents the sight,
I see no fears:
Thy hand is white,
Thy scales like buckets, which attend
And interchangeably descend,
Lifting to heaven from this well of tears.

For where before thou still didst call on me,
Now I still touch
And harp on thee.
Gods promises have made thee mine;
Why should I justice now decline?
Against me there is none, but for me much.

THE PILGRIMAGE

I TRAVELL'D on, seeing the hill, where lay
My expectation.
A long it was and weary way.
The gloomy cave of Desperation
I left on th' one, and on the other side
The rock of Pride.

And so I came to phansies medow strow'd
With many a flower:
Fain would I here have made abode,
But I was quicken'd by my houre.
So to cares cops I came, and there got through
With much ado.

That led me to the wilde of passion, which
Some call the wold;
A wasted place, but sometimes rich.
Here I was robb'd of all my gold,
Save one good Angell, which a friend had ti'd
Close to my side.

At length I got unto the gladsome hill,
Where lay my hope,
Where lay my heart; and climbing still,
When I had gain'd the brow and top,
A lake of brackish waters on the ground
Was all I found.

With that abash'd and struck with many a sting
Of swarming fears,
I fell, and cry'd, Alas my King;
Can both the way and end be tears?
Yet taking heart I rose, and then perceiv'd
I was deceiv'd:

My hill was further: so I flung away,
Yet heard a crie
Just as I went, *None goes that way*
And lives: If that be all, said I,
After so foul a journey death is fair,
And but a chair.

THE HOLDFAST

I THREATNED to observe the strict decree
Of my deare God with all my power and might.
But I was told by one, it could not be;
Yet I might trust in God to be my light.

Then will I trust, said I, in him alone.
Nay, ev'n to trust in him, was also his:
We must confesse, that nothing is our own.
Then I confesse that he my succour is:

But to have nought is ours, not to confesse
That we have nought. I stood amaz'd at this,
Much troubled, till I heard a friend expresse,
That all things were more ours by being his.
What Adam had, and forfeited for all,
Christ keepeth now, who cannot fail or fall.

COMPLAINING

Do not beguile my heart,
Because thou art
My power and wisdome. Put me not to shame,
Because I am
Thy clay that weeps, thy dust that calls.

Thou art the Lord of glorie;
The deed and storie
Are both thy due: but I a silly flie,
That live or die
According as the weather falls.

Art thou all justice, Lord?
Shows not thy word
More attributes? Am I all throat or eye,
To weep or crie?
Have I no parts but those of grief?

Let not thy wrathfull power
Afflict my houre,
My inch of life: or let thy gracious power
Contract my houre,
That I may climbe and finde relief.

THE DISCHARGE

Busie enquiring heart, what wouldst thou know?
Why dost thou prie,
And turn, and leer, and with a licorous eye
Look high and low;
And in thy lookings stretch and grow?

Hast thou not made thy counts, and summ'd up all?
Did not thy heart
Give up the whole, and with the whole depart?
Let what will fall:
That which is past who can recall?

Thy life is Gods, thy time to come is gone,
And is his right.
He is thy night at noon: he is at night
Thy noon alone.
The crop is his, for he hath sown.

And well it was for thee, when this befell,
That God did make
Thy businesse his, and in thy life partake:
For thou canst tell,
If it be his once, all is well.

Onely the present is thy part and fee.
And happy thou,
If, though thou didst not beat thy future brow,
Thou couldst well see
What present things requir'd of thee.

They ask enough; why shouldst thou further go?
Raise not the mudde
Of future depths, but drink the cleare and good.
Dig not for wo
In times to come; for it will grow.

Man and the present fit: if he provide,
He breaks the square.
This houre is mine: if for the next I care,
I grow too wide,
And do encroach upon deaths side.

For death each houre environs and surrounds.
He that would know
And care for future chances, cannot go
Unto those grounds, [boũds.
But through a Church-yard which thẽ

Things present shrink and die: but they that spend
Their thoughts and sense
On future grief, do not remove it thence,
But it extend,
And draw the bottome out an end.

God chains the dog till night: wilt loose the chain,
And wake thy sorrow?
Wilt thou forestall it, and now grieve to morrow,
And then again
Grieve over freshly all thy pain?

Either grief will not come: or if it must,
Do not forecast.
And while it cometh, it is almost past.
Away distrust:
My God hath promis'd, he is just.

PRAISE

King of Glorie, King of Peace,
I will love thee:
And that love may never cease,
I will move thee.

Thou hast granted my request,
Thou hast heard me:
Thou didst note my working breast,
Thou hast spar'd me.

Wherefore with my utmost art
I will sing thee,
And the cream of all my heart
I will bring thee.

Though my sinnes against me cried,
Thou didst cleare me;
And alone, when they replied,
Thou didst heare me.

Sev'n whole dayes, not one in seven,
I will praise thee.
In my heart, though not in heaven,
I can raise thee.

Thou grew'st soft and moist with tears,
Thou relentedst:
And when Justice call'd for fears,
Thou dissentedst.

Small it is, in this poore sort
To enroll thee:
Ev'n eternitie is too short
To extoll thee.

AN OFFERING

Come, bring thy gift. If blessings were as slow
As mens returns, what would become of fools?
What hast thou there? a heart? but is it pure?
Search well and see; for hearts have many holes.
Yet one pure heart is nothing to bestow:
In Christ two natures met to be thy cure.

O that within us hearts had propagation,
Since many gifts do challenge many hearts!
Yet one, if good, may title to a number;
And single things grow fruitfull by deserts.
In publick judgements one may be a nation,
And fence a plague, while others sleep and slumber.

But all I fear is lest thy heart displease,
As neither good, nor one: so oft divisions
Thy lusts have made, and not thy lusts alone;
Thy passions also have their set partitions.
These parcell out thy heart: recover these,
And thou mayst offer many gifts in one.

There is a balsome, or indeed a bloud, [close
Dropping from heav'n, which doth both cleanse and
All sorts of wounds; of such strange force it is.
Seek out this All-heal, and seek no repose,
Untill thou finde and use it to thy good:
Then bring thy gift; and let thy hymne be this;

Since my sadnesse
Into gladnesse
Lord thou dost convert,
O accept
What thou hast kept,
As thy due desert.

Had I many,
Had I any,
(For this heart is none)
All were thine
And none of mine:
Surely thine alone.

Yet thy favour
May give savour
To this poore oblation;
And it raise
To be thy praise,
And be my salvation.

LONGING

WITH sick and famisht eyes,
With doubling knees and weary bones,
To thee my cries,
To thee my grones,
To thee my sighs, my tears ascend:
No end?

My throat, my soul is hoarse;
My heart is wither'd like a ground
Which thou dost curse.
My thoughts turn round,
And make me giddie; Lord, I fall,
Yet call.

From thee all pitie flows.
Mothers are kinde, because thou art,
And dost dispose
To them a part:
Their infants, them; and they suck thee
More free.

Bowels of pitie, heare!
Lord of my soul, love of my minde,
Bow down thine eare!
Let not the winde
Scatter my words, and in the same
Thy name!

LONGING

Look on my sorrows round!
Mark well my furnace! O what flames,
What heats abound!
What griefs, what shames!
Consider, Lord; Lord, bow thine eare,
And heare!

Lord Jesu, thou didst bow
Thy dying head upon the tree:
O be not now
More dead to me!
Lord heare! *Shall he that made the eare,*
Not heare?

Behold, thy dust doth stirre,
It moves, it creeps, it aims at thee:
Wilt thou deferre
To succour me,
Thy pile of dust, wherein each crumme
Sayes, Come?

To thee help appertains.
Hast thou left all things to their course,
And laid the reins
Upon the horse?
Is all lockt? hath a sinners plea
No key?

Indeed the world's thy book,
Where all things have their leafe assign'd:
Yet a meek look
Hath interlin'd.
Thy board is full, yet humble guests
Finde nests.

Thou tarriest, while I die,
And fall to nothing: thou dost reigne,
And rule on high,
While I remain
In bitter grief: yet am I stil'd
Thy childe.

Lord, didst thou leave thy throne,
Not to relieve? how can it be,
That thou art grown
Thus hard to me?
Were sinne alive, good cause there were
To bear.

But now both sinne is dead,
And all thy promises live and bide.
That wants his head;
These speak and chide,
And in thy bosom poure my tears,
As theirs.

Lord Jesu, heare my heart,
Which hath been broken now so long,
That ev'ry part
Hath got a tongue!
Thy beggars grow; rid them away
To day.

My love, my sweetnesse, heare!
By these thy feet, at which my heart
Lies all the yeare,
Pluck out thy dart,
And heal my troubled breast which cryes,
Which dyes.

THE BAG

Away despair; my gracious Lord doth heare.
    Though windes and waves assault my keel,
    He doth preserve it: he doth steer,
    Ev'n when the boat seems most to reel.
    Storms are the triumph of his art:
Well may he close his eyes, but not his heart.

Hast thou not heard, that my Lord Jesus di'd?
    Then let me tell thee a strange storie.
    The God of power, as he did ride
    In his majestick robes of glorie,
    Resolv'd to light; and so one day
He did descend, undressing all the way.

The starres his tire of light and rings obtain'd,
    The cloud his bow, the fire his spear,
    The sky his azure mantle gain'd.
    And when they ask'd, what he would wear;
    He smil'd and said as he did go,
He had new clothes a making here below.

When he was come, as travellers are wont,
    He did repair unto an inne.
    Both then, and after, many a brunt
    He did endure to cancell sinne:
    And having giv'n the rest before,
Here he gave up his life to pay our score.

But as he was returning, there came one
That ran upon him with a spear.
He, who came hither all alone,
Bringing nor man, nor arms, nor fear,
Receiv'd the blow upon his side,
And straight he turn'd, and to his brethren cry'd,

If ye have any thing to send or write,
(I have no bag, but here is room)
Unto my fathers hands and sight
(Beleeve me) it shall safely come,
That I shall minde, what you impart;
Look, you may put it very neare my heart.

Or if hereafter any of my friends
Will use me in this kinde, the doore
Shall still be open; what he sends
I will present, and somewhat more,
Not to his hurt. Sighs will convey
Any thing to me. Heark despair, away.

THE JEWS

POORE nation, whose sweet sap, and juice
Our cyens have purloin'd, and left you drie:
Whose streams we got by the Apostles sluce,
And use in baptisme, while ye pine and die:
Who by not keeping once, became a debter;
And now by keeping lose the letter:

Oh that my prayers! mine, alas!
Oh that some Angel might a trumpet sound;
At which the Church falling upon her face
Should crie so loud, until the trump were drown'd,
And by that crie of her deare Lord obtain,
That your sweet sap might come again!

THE COLLAR

I STRUCK the board, and cry'd, No more.
I will abroad.
What? shall I ever sigh and pine?
My lines and life are free; free as the rode,
Loose as the winde, as large as store.
Shall I be still in suit?
Have I no harvest but a thorn
To let me bloud, and not restore
What I have lost with cordiall fruit?
Sure there was wine
Before my sighs did drie it: there was corn
Before my tears did drown it.
Is the yeare onely lost to me?
Have I no bayes to crown it?
No flowers, no garlands gay? all blasted?
All wasted?
Not so, my heart: but there is fruit,
And thou hast hands.
Recover all thy sigh-blown age
On double pleasures: leave thy cold dispute
Of what is fit, and not forsake thy cage,
Thy rope of sands,

Which pettie thoughts have made, and made to thee
Good cable, to enforce and draw,
And be thy law,
While thou didst wink and wouldst not see.
Away; take heed:
I will abroad.
Call in thy deaths head there: tie up thy fears.
He that forbears
To suit and serve his need,
Deserves his load.
But as I rav'd and grew more fierce and wilde
At every word,
Me thoughts I heard one calling, *Childe:*
And I reply'd, *My Lord.*

THE GLIMPSE

WHITHER away delight?
Thou cam'st but now; wilt thou so soon depart,
And give me up to night?
For many weeks of lingring pain and smart
But one half houre of comfort for my heart?

Me thinks delight should have
More skill in musick, and keep better time.
Wert thou a winde or wave,
They quickly go and come with lesser crime:
Flowers look about, and die not in their prime.

Thy short abode and stay
Feeds not, but addes to the desire of meat.
Lime begg'd of old (they say)
A neighbour spring to cool his inward heat;
Which by the springs accesse grew much more great.

In hope of thee my heart
Pickt here and there a crumme, and would not die ;
But constant to his part
When as my fears foretold this, did replie,
A slender thread a gentle guest will tie.

Yet if the heart that wept
Must let thee go, return when it doth knock.
Although thy heap be kept
For future times, the droppings of the stock
May oft break forth, and never break the lock.

If I have more to spinne,
The wheel shall go, so that thy stay be short.
Thou knowst how grief and sinne
Disturb the work. O make me not their sport,
Who by thy coming may be made a court!

ASSURANCE

O SPITEFUL bitter thought!
Bitterly spiteful thought! Couldst thou invent
So high a torture? Is such poyson bought?
Doubtlesse, but in the way of punishment,
When wit contrives to meet with thee,
No such rank poyson can there be.

Thou said'st but even now,
That all was not so fair, as I conceiv'd,
Betwixt my God and me; that I allow
And coin large hopes; but, that I was deceiv'd:
Either the league was broke, or neare it;
And, that I had great cause to fear it.

And what to this? what more
Could poyson, if it had a tongue, expresse?
What is thy aim? wouldst thou unlock the doore
To cold despairs, and gnawing pensivenesse?
Wouldst thou raise devils? I see, I know,
I writ thy purpose long ago.

But I will to my Father,
Who heard thee say it. O most gracious Lord,
If all the hope and comfort that I gather,
Were from my self, I had not half a word,
Not half a letter to oppose
What is objected by my foes.

But thou art my desert:
And in this league, which now my foes invade,
Thou art not onely to perform thy part,
But also mine; as when the league was made
Thou didst at once thy self indite,
And hold my hand, while I did write.

Wherefore if thou canst fail,
Then can thy truth and I: but while rocks stand,
And rivers stirre, thou canst not shrink or quail:
Yea, when both rocks and all things shall disband,
Then shalt thou be my rock and tower,
And make their ruine praise thy power.

Now foolish thought go on,
Spin out thy thread, and make thereof a coat
To hide thy shame: for thou hast cast a bone
Which bounds on thee, and will not down thy throat:
What for it self love once began,
Now love and truth will end in man.

THE CALL

Come, my Way, my Truth, my Life:
Such a Way, as gives us breath:
Such a Truth, as ends all strife:
And such a Life, as killeth death.

Come, my Light, my Feast, my Strength:
Such a Light, as shows a feast:
Such a Feast, as mends in length:
Such a Strength, as makes his guest.

Come, my Joy, my Love, my Heart:
Such a Joy, as none can move:
Such a Love, as none can part:
Such a Heart, as joyes in love.

CLASPING OF HANDS

Lord, thou art mine, and I am thine,
If mine I am: and thine much more,
Then I or ought, or can be mine.
Yet to be thine, doth me restore;
So that again I now am mine,
And with advantage mine the more.
Since this being mine, brings with it thine,
And thou with me dost thee restore.
　　If I without thee would be mine,
　　I neither should be mine nor thine.

Lord, I am thine, and thou art mine:
So mine thou art, that something more
I may presume thee mine, then thine.
For thou didst suffer to restore
Not thee, but me, and to be mine:
And with advantage mine the more,
Since thou in death wast none of thine,
Yet then as mine didst me restore.
O be mine still! still make me thine!
Or rather make no Thine and Mine!

PRAISE

Lord, I will mean and speak thy praise,
Thy praise alone.
My busie heart shall spin it all my dayes:
And when it stops for want of store,
Then will I wring it with a sigh or grone,
That thou mayst yet have more.

When thou dost favour any action,
It runnes, it flies:
All things concurre to give it a perfection.
That which had but two legs before,
When thou dost blesse, hath twelve: one wheel doth rise
To twentie then, or more.

But when thou dost on businesse blow,
It hangs, it clogs:
Not all the teams of Albion in a row
Can hale or draw it out of doore.
Legs are but stumps, and Pharaohs wheels but logs,
And struggling hinders more.

PRAISE

Thousands of things do thee employ
In ruling all
This spacious globe: Angels must have their joy,
Devils their rod, the sea his shore,
The windes their stint: and yet when I did call,
Thou heardst my call, and more.

I have not lost one single tear:
But when mine eyes
Did weep to heav'n, they found a bottle there
(As we have boxes for the poore)
Readie to take them in; yet of a size
That would contain much more.

But after thou hadst slipt a drop
From thy right eye,
(Which there did hang like streamers neare the top
Of some fair church to show the sore
And bloudie battell which thou once didst trie)
The glasse was full and more.

Wherefore I sing. Yet since my heart,
Though press'd, runnes thin;
O that I might some other hearts convert,
And so take up at use good store:
That to thy chests there might be coming in
Both all my praise, and more!

JOSEPHS COAT

Wounded I sing, tormented I indite,
Thrown down I fall into a bed, and rest:
Sorrow hath chang'd its note: such is his will,
Who changeth all things, as him pleaseth best.
    For well he knows, if but one grief and smart
Among my many had his full career,
Sure it would carrie with it ev'n my heart,
And both would runne untill they found a biere
    To fetch the bodie; both being due to grief.
But he hath spoil'd the race; and giv'n to anguish
One of Joyes coats, ticing it with relief
To linger in me, and together languish.
    I live to shew his power, who once did bring
    My *joyes* to *weep*, and now my *griefs* to *sing*.

THE PULLEY

    When God at first made man,
Having a glasse of blessings standing by;
Let us (said he) poure on him all we can:
Let the worlds riches, which dispersed lie,
    Contract into a span.

    So strength first made a way;
Then beautie flow'd, then wisdome, honour, pleasure:
When almost all was out, God made a stay,
Perceiving that alone of all his treasure
    Rest in the bottome lay.

For if I should (said he)
Bestow this jewell also on my creature,
He would adore my gifts in stead of me,
And rest in Nature, not the God of Nature.
So both should losers be.

Yet let him keep the rest,
But keep them with repining restlessnesse:
Let him be rich and wearie, that at least,
If goodnesse leade him not, yet wearinesse
May tosse him to my breast.

THE PRIESTHOOD

Blest Order, which in power dost so excell,
That with th' one hand thou liftest to the sky,
And with the other throwest down to hell
In thy just censures; fain would I draw nigh,
Fain put thee on, exchanging my lay-sword
For that of th' holy word.

But thou art fire, sacred and hallow'd fire;
And I but earth and clay: should I presume
To wear thy habit, the severe attire
My slender compositions might consume.
I am both foul and brittle; much unfit
To deal in holy Writ.

Yet have I often seen, by cunning hand
And force of fire, what curious things are made
Of wretched earth. Where once I scorn'd to stand,
That earth is fitted by the fire and trade
Of skilfull artists, for the boards of those
Who make the bravest shows.

But since those great ones, be they ne're so great,
Come from the earth, from whence those vessels come;
So that at once both feeder, dish, and meat
Have one beginning and one finall summe:
I do not greatly wonder at the sight,
If earth in earth delight.

But th' holy men of God such vessels are,
As serve him up, who all the world commands:
When God vouchsafeth to become our fare,
Their hands conuey him, who conveys their hands.
O what pure things, most pure must those things be,
Who bring my God to me!

Wherefore I dare not, I, put forth my hand
To hold the Ark, although it seem to shake
Through th' old sinnes and new doctrines of our land.
Onely, since God doth often vessels make
Of lowly matter for high uses meet,
I throw me at his feet.

There will I lie, untill my Maker seek
For some mean stuffe whereon to show his skill:
Then is my time. The distance of the meek
Doth flatter power. Lest good come short of ill
In praising might, the poore do by submission
What pride by opposition.

THE SEARCH

WHITHER, O, whither art thou fled,
My Lord, My Love?
My searches are my daily bread;
Yet never prove.

THE SEARCH

My knees pierce th' earth, mine eies the skie;
And yet the sphere
And centre both to me denie
That thou art there.

Yet can I mark how herbs below
Grow green and gay,
As if to meet thee they did know,
While I decay.

Yet can I mark how starres above
Simper and shine,
As having keyes unto thy love,
While poore I pine.

I sent a sigh to seek thee out,
Deep drawn in pain,
Wing'd like an arrow: but my scout
Returns in vain.

I tun'd another (having store)
Into a grone;
Because the search was dumbe before:
But all was one.

Lord, dost thou some new fabrick mold
Which favour winnes,
And keeps thee present, leaving th' old
Unto their sinnes?

Where is my God? what hidden place
Conceals thee still?
What covert dare eclipse thy face?
Is it thy will?

O let not that of any thing;
Let rather brasse,
Or steel, or mountains be thy ring,
And I will passe.

Thy will such an intrenching is,
As passeth thought:
To it all strength, all subtilties
Are things of nought.

Thy will such a strange distance is,
As that to it
East and West touch, the poles do kisse,
And parallels meet.

Since then my grief must be as large,
As is thy space,
Thy distance from me; see my charge,
Lord, see my case.

O take these barres, these lengths away;
Turn, and restore me:
Be not Almightie, let me say,
Against, but for me.

When thou dost turn, and wilt be neare;
What edge so keen,
What point so piercing can appeare
To come between?

For as thy absence doth excell
All distance known:
So doth thy nearenesse bear the bell,
Making two one.

GRIEF

O WHO will give me tears? Come all ye springs,
Dwell in my head & eyes: come clouds, & rain:
My grief hath need of all the watry things,
That nature hath produc'd. Let ev'ry vein
Suck up a river to supply mine eyes,
My weary weeping eyes too drie for me,
Unlesse they get new conduits, new supplies
To beare them out, and with my state agree.
What are two shallow foords, two little spouts
Of a lesse world? the greater is but small,
A narrow cupboard for my griefs and doubts,
Which want provision in the midst of all.
Verses, ye are too fine a thing, too wise
For my rough sorrows: cease, be dumbe and mute,
Give up your feet and running to mine eyes,
And keep your measures for some lovers lute,
Whose grief allows him musick and a ryme:
For mine excludes both measure, tune, and time.
Alas, my God!

THE CROSSE

WHAT is this strange and uncouth thing?
To make me sigh, and seek, and faint, and die,
Untill I had some place, where I might sing,
And serve thee; and not onely I,
But all my wealth, and familie might combine
To set thy honour up, as our designe.

And then when after much delay,
Much wrastling, many a combate, this deare end,
So much desir'd, is giv'n, to take away
My power to serve thee; to unbend
All my abilities, my designes confound,
And lay my threatnings bleeding on the ground.

One ague dwelleth in my bones,
Another in my soul (the memorie
What I would do for thee, if once my grones
Could be allow'd for harmonie)
I am in all a weak disabled thing,
Save in the sight thereof, where strength doth sting.

Besides, things sort not to my will,
Ev'n when my will doth studie thy renown:
Thou turnest th' edge of all things on me still,
Taking me up to throw me down:
So that, ev'n when my hopes seem to be sped,
I am to grief alive, to them as dead.

To have my aim, and yet to be
Further from it then when I bent my bow;
To make my hopes my torture, and the fee
Of all my woes another wo,
Is in the midst of delicates to need,
And ev'n in Paradise to be a weed.

Ah my deare Father, ease my smart!
These contrarieties crush me: these crosse actions
Doe winde a rope about, and cut my heart:
And yet since these thy contradictions
Are properly a crosse felt by thy sonne,
With but foure words, my words, *Thy will be done.*

THE FLOWER

How fresh, O Lord, how sweet and clean
Are thy returns! ev'n as the flowers in spring;
To which, besides their own demean,
The late-past frosts tributes of pleasure bring.
Grief melts away
Like snow in May,
As if there were no such cold thing.

Who would have thought my shrivel'd heart
Could have recover'd greennesse? It was gone
Quite under ground; as flowers depart
To see their mother-root, when they have blown;
Where they together
All the hard weather,
Dead to the world, keep house unknown.

These are thy wonders, Lord of power,
Killing and quickning, bringing down to hell
And up to heaven in an houre;
Making a chiming of a passing-bell.
We say amisse,
This or that is:
Thy word is all, if we could spell.

O that I once past changing were,
Fast in thy Paradise, where no flower can wither!
Many a spring I shoot up fair,
Offring at heav'n, growing and groning thither:
Nor doth my flower
Want a spring-showre,
My sinnes and I joining together:

But while I grow in a straight line,
Still upwards bent, as if heav'n were mine own,
Thy anger comes, and I decline:
What frost to that? what pole is not the zone,
Where all things burn,
When thou dost turn,
And the least frown of thine is shown?

And now in age I bud again,
After so many deaths I live and write;
I once more smell the dew and rain,
And relish versing: O my onely light,
It cannot be
That I am he
On whom thy tempests fell all night.

These are thy wonders, Lord of love,
To make us see we are but flowers that glide:
Which when we once can finde and prove,
Thou hast a garden for us, where to bide.
Who would be more,
Swelling through store,
Forfeit their Paradise by their pride.

DOTAGE

False glozing pleasures, casks of happinesse,
Foolish night-fires, womens and childrens wishes,
Chases in Arras, guilded emptinesse,
Shadows well mounted, dreams in a career,
Embroider'd lyes, nothing between two dishes;
These are the pleasures here.

THE SONNE

True earnest sorrows, rooted miseries,
Anguish in grain, vexations ripe and blown,
Sure-footed griefs, solid calamities,
Plain demonstrations, evident and cleare,
Fetching their proofs ev'n from the very bone;
These are the sorrows here.

But oh the folly of distracted men,
Who griefs in earnest, joyes in jest pursue;
Preferring, like brute beasts, a lothsome den
Before a court, ev'n that above so cleare,
Where are no sorrows, but delights more true,
Then miseries are here!

THE SONNE

Let forrain nations of their language boast,
What fine varietie each tongue affords:
I like our language, as our men and coast:
Who cannot dresse it well, want wit, not words.
How neatly doe we give one onely name
To parents issue and the sunnes bright starre!
A sonne is light and fruit; a fruitfull flame
Chasing the fathers dimnesse, carri'd farre
From the first man in th' East, to fresh and new
Western discov'ries of posteritie.
So in one word our Lords humilitie
We turn upon him in a sense most true:
For what Christ once in humblenesse began,
We him in glorie call, *The Sonne of Man.*

A TRUE HYMNE

My joy, my life, my crown!
My heart was meaning all the day,
Somewhat it fain would say:
And still it runneth mutt'ring up and down
With onely this, *My joy, my life, my crown.*

Yet slight not these few words:
If truly said, they may take part
Among the best in art.
The finenesse which a hymne or psalme affords,
Is, when the soul unto the lines accords.

He who craves all the minde,
And all the soul, and strength, and time,
If the words onely ryme,
Justly complains, that somewhat is behinde
To make his verse, or write a hymne in kinde.

Whereas if th' heart be moved,
Although the verse be somewhat scant,
God doth supplie the want.
As when th' heart sayes (sighing to be approved)
O, could I love! and stops: God writeth, *Loved.*

THE ANSWER

My comforts drop and melt away like snow:
I shake my head, and all the thoughts and ends,
Which my fierce youth did bandie, fall and flow
Like leaves about me; or like summer friends,

Flyes of estates and sunne-shine. But to all,
Who think me eager, hot, and undertaking,
But in my prosecutions slack and small;
As a young exhalation, newly waking,
Scorns his first bed of dirt, and means the sky;
But cooling by the way, grows pursie and slow,
And setling to a cloud, doth live and die
In that dark state of tears: to all, that so
    Show me, and set me, I have one reply,
Which they that know the rest, know more then I.

A DIALOGUE-ANTHEME

Christian. Death.

Chr. ALAS, poore Death, where is thy glorie?
    Where is thy famous force, thy ancient sting?
Dea. *Alas poore mortall, void of storie,*
    Go spell and reade how I have kill'd thy King.
Chr. Poore death! and who was hurt thereby?
    Thy curse being laid on him, makes thee accurst.
Dea. *Let losers talk: yet thou shalt die;*
    These arms shall crush thee. *Chr.* Spare not, do thy worst.
    I shall be one day better then before:
    Thou so much worse, that thou shalt be no more.

THE WATER-COURSE

Thou who dost dwell and linger here below,
Since the condition of this world is frail,
Where of all plants afflictions soonest grow;
If troubles overtake thee, do not wail:
For who can look for lesse, that loveth { Life. / Strife.

But rather turn the pipe, and waters course
To serve thy sinnes, and furnish thee with store
Of sov'raigne tears, springing from true remorse:
That so in purenesse thou mayst him adore,
Who gives to man, as he sees fit { Salvation. / Damnation.

SELF-CONDEMNATION

Thou who condemnest Jewish hate,
For choosing Barabbas a murderer
Before the Lord of glorie;
Look back upon thine own estate,
Call home thine eye (that busie wanderer)
That choice may be thy storie.

He that doth love, and love amisse
This worlds delights before true Christian joy,
Hath made a Jewish choice:
The world an ancient murderer is;
Thousands of souls it hath and doth destroy
With her enchanting voice.

He that hath made a sorrie wedding
Between his soul and gold, and hath preferr'd
False gain before the true,
Hath done what he condemnes in reading:
For he hath sold for money his deare Lord,
And is a Judas-Jew.

Thus we prevent the last great day,
And judge our selves. That light, which sin & passion
Did before dimme and choke,
When once those snuffes are ta'ne away,
Shines bright and cleare, ev'n unto condemnation,
Without excuse or cloke.

BITTER-SWEET

Ah my deare angrie Lord,
Since thou dost love, yet strike;
Cast down, yet help afford;
Sure I will do the like.
I will complain, yet praise;
I will bewail, approve:
And all my sowre-sweet dayes
I will lament, and love.

THE GLANCE

When first thy sweet and gracious eye
Vouchsaf'd ev'n in the midst of youth and night
To look upon me, who before did lie
Weltring in sinne;

I felt a sugred strange delight,
Passing all cordials made by any art,
Bedew, embalme, and overrunne my heart,
And take it in.

Since that time many a bitter storm
My soul hath felt, ev'n able to destroy,
Had the malicious and ill-meaning harm
His swing and sway:
But still thy sweet originall joy
Sprung from thine eye, did work within my soul,
And surging griefs, when they grew bold, controll,
And got the day.

If thy first glance so powerfull be,
A mirth but open'd and seal'd up again;
What wonders shall we feel, when we shall see
Thy full-ey'd love!
When thou shalt look us out of pain,
And one aspect of thine spend in delight
More then a thousand sunnes disburse in light,
In heav'n above.

THE 23 PSALME

THE God of love my shepherd is,
And he that doth me feed:
While he is mine, and I am his,
What can I want or need?

He leads me to the tender grasse,
Where I both feed and rest;
Then to the streams that gently passe:
In both I have the best.

Or if I stray, he doth convert
And bring my minde in frame:
And all this not for my desert,
But for his holy name.

Yea, in deaths shadie black abode
Well may I walk, not fear:
For thou art with me; and thy rod
To guide, thy staffe to bear.

Nay, thou dost make me sit and dine,
Ev'n in my enemies sight:
My head with oyl, my cup with wine
Runnes over day and night.

Surely thy sweet and wondrous love
Shall measure all my dayes;
And as it never shall remove,
So neither shall my praise.

MARIE MAGDALENE

When blessed Marie wip'd her Saviours feet,
(Whose precepts she had trampled on before)
And wore them for a jewell on her head,
Shewing his steps should be the street,
Wherein she thenceforth evermore
With pensive humblenesse would live and tread:

She being stain'd her self, why did she strive
To make him clean, who could not be defil'd?
Why kept she not her tears for her own faults,
And not his feet? Though we could dive
In tears like seas, our sinnes are pil'd
Deeper then they, in words, and works, and thoughts.

Deare soul, she knew who did vouchsafe and deigne
To bear her filth; and that her sinnes did dash
Ev'n God himself: wherefore she was not loth,
As she had brought wherewith to stain,
So to bring in wherewith to wash:
And yet in washing one, she washed both.

AARON

Holinesse on the head,
Light and perfections on the breast,
Harmonious bells below, raising the dead
To leade them unto life and rest.
Thus are true Aarons drest.

Profanenesse in my head,
Defects and darknesse in my breast,
A noise of passions ringing me for dead
Unto a place where is no rest,
Poore priest thus am I drest.

Onely another head
I have, another heart and breast,
Another musick, making live not dead,
Without whom I could have no rest:
In him I am well drest.

Christ is my onely head,
My alone onely heart and breast,
My onely musick, striking me ev'n dead;
That to the old man I may rest,
And be in him new drest.

So holy in my head,
Perfect and light in my deare breast,
My doctrine tun'd by Christ, (who is not dead,
But lives in me while I do rest)
Come people; Aaron's drest.

THE ODOUR

2 Cor. II.

How sweetly doth *My Master* sound! *My Master!*
As Amber-greese leaves a rich sent
Unto the taster:
So do these words a sweet content,
An orientall fragrancie, *My Master.*

With these all day I do perfume my minde,
My minde ev'n thrust into them both:
That I might finde
What cordials make this curious broth,
This broth of smells, that feeds and fats my minde.

My Master, shall I speak? O that to thee
My servant were a little so,
As flesh may be;
That these two words might creep & [grow
To some degree of spicinesse to thee!

Then should the Pomander, which was before
A speaking sweet, mend by reflection,
And tell me more:
For pardon of my imperfection
Would warm and work it sweeter then before.

For when *My Master*, which alone is sweet,
And ev'n in my unworthinesse pleasing,
Shall call and meet,
My servant, as thee not displeasing,
That call is but the breathing of the sweet.

This breathing would with gains by sweetning me
(As sweet things traffick when they meet)
Return to thee.
And so this new commerce and sweet
Should all my life employ, and busie me.

THE FOIL

If we could see below
The sphere of vertue, and each shining grace
As plainly as that above doth show;
This were the better skie, the brighter place.

God hath made starres the foil
To set off vertues; griefs to set off sinning:
Yet in this wretched world we toil,
As if grief were not foul, nor vertue winning.

THE FORERUNNERS

THE harbingers are come. See, see their mark;
White is their colour, and behold my head.
But must they have my brain? must they dispark
Those sparkling notions, which therein were bred?
        Must dulnesse turn me to a clod?
Yet have they left me, *Thou art still my God.*

Good men ye be, to leave me my best room,
Ev'n all my heart, and what is lodged there:
I passe not, I, what of the rest become,
So *Thou art still my God*, be out of fear.
        He will be pleased with that dittie;
And if I please him, I write fine and wittie.

Farewell sweet phrases, lovely metaphors.
But will ye leave me thus? when ye before
Of stews and brothels onely knew the doores,
Then did I wash you with my tears, and more,
        Brought you to Church well drest and clad:
My God must have my best, ev'n all I had.

Louely enchanting language, sugar-cane,
Hony of roses, whither wilt thou flie?
Hath some fond lover tic'd thee to thy bane?
And wilt thou leave the Church, and love a stie?
        Fie, thou wilt soil thy broider'd coat,
And hurt thy self, and him that sings the note.

Let foolish lovers, if they will love dung,
With canvas, not with arras clothe their shame:
Let follie speak in her own native tongue.
True beautie dwells on high: ours is a flame
  But borrow'd thence to light us thither.
Beautie and beauteous words should go together.

Yet if you go, I passe not; take your way:
For, *Thou art still my God*, is all that ye
Perhaps with more embellishment can say,
Go birds of spring: let winter have his fee,
  Let a bleak palenesse chalk the doore,
So all within be livelier then before.

THE ROSE

Presse me not to take more pleasure
  In this world of sugred lies,
And to use a larger measure
  Then my strict, yet welcome size.

First, there is no pleasure here:
  Colour'd griefs indeed there are,
Blushing woes, that look as cleare
  As if they could beautie spare.

Or if such deceits there be,
  Such delights I meant to say;
There are no such things to me,
  Who have pass'd my right away.

But I will not much oppose
Unto what you now advise:
Onely take this gentle rose,
And therein my answer lies.

What is fairer then a rose?
What is sweeter? yet it purgeth.
Purgings enmitie disclose,
Enmitie forbearance urgeth.

If then all that worldlings prize
Be contracted to a rose;
Sweetly there indeed it lies,
But it biteth in the close.

So this flower doth judge and sentence
Worldly joyes to be a scourge:
For they all produce repentance,
And repentance is a purge.

But I health, not physick choose:
Onely though I you oppose,
Say that fairly I refuse,
For my answer is a rose.

DISCIPLINE

Throw away thy rod,
Throw away thy wrath:
O my God,
Take the gentle path.

For my hearts desire
Unto thine is bent:
                    I aspire
To a full consent.

Not a word or look
I affect to own,
                    But by book,
And thy book alone.

Though I fail, I weep:
Though I halt in pace,
                    Yet I creep
To the throne of grace.

Then let wrath remove;
Love will do the deed:
                    For with love
Stonie hearts will bleed.

Love is swift of foot;
Love's a man of warre,
                    And can shoot,
And can hit from farre.

Who can scape his bow?
That which wrought on thee,
                    Brought thee low,
Needs must work on me.

Throw away thy rod;
Though man frailties hath,
                    Thou art God:
Throw away thy wrath.

THE INVITATION

COME ye hither all, whose taste
Is your waste;
Save your cost, and mend your fare.
God is here prepar'd and drest,
And the feast,
God, in whom all dainties are.

Come ye hither all, whom wine
Doth define,
Naming you not to your good:
Weep what ye have drunk amisse,
And drink this,
Which before ye drink is bloud.

Come ye hither all, whom pain
Doth arraigne,
Bringing all your sinnes to sight:
Taste and fear not: God is here
In this cheer,
And on sinne doth cast the fright.

Come ye hither all, whom joy
Doth destroy,
While ye graze without your bounds:
Here is joy that drowneth quite
Your delight,
As a floud the lower grounds.

Come ye hither all, whose love
Is your dove,
And exalts you to the skie:
Here is love, which having breath
Ev'n in death,
After death can never die.

Lord I have invited all,
And I shall
Still invite, still call to thee:
For it seems but just and right
In my sight,
Where is all, there all should be.

THE BANQUET

Welcome sweet and sacred cheer,
Welcome deare;
With me, in me, live and dwell:
For thy neatnesse passeth sight,
Thy delight
Passeth tongue to taste or tell.

O what sweetnesse from the bowl
Fills my soul,
Such as is, and makes divine!
Is some starre (fled from the sphere)
Melted there,
As we sugar melt in wine?

Or hath sweetnesse in the bread
Made a head
To subdue the smell of sinne;
Flowers, and gummes, and powders giving
All their living,
Lest the enemie should winne?

Doubtlesse, neither starre nor flower
Hath the power
Such a sweetnesse to impart:
Onely God, who gives perfumes,
Flesh assumes,
And with it perfumes my heart.

But as Pomanders and wood
Still are good,
Yet being bruis'd are better sented:
God, to show how farre his love
Could improve,
Here, as broken, is presented.

When I had forgot my birth,
And on earth
In delights of earth was drown'd;
God took bloud, and needs would be
Spilt with me,
And so found me on the ground.

Having rais'd me to look up,
In a cup
Sweetly he doth meet my taste.
But I still being low and short,
Farre from court,
Wine becomes a wing at last.

For with it alone I flie
To the skie:
Where I wipe mine eyes, and see
What I seek, for what I sue;
Him I view,
Who hath done so much for me.

Let the wonder of this pitie
Be my dittie,
And take up my lines and life:
Hearken under pain of death,
Hands and breath;
Strive in this, and love the strife.

THE POSIE

Let wits contest,
And with their words and posies windows fill:
Lesse then the least
Of all thy mercies, is my posie still.

This on my ring,
This by my picture, in my book I write:
Whether I sing,
Or say, or dictate, this is my delight.

Invention rest,
Comparisons go play, wit use thy will:
Lesse then the least
Of all Gods mercies, is my posie still.

A PARODIE

Souls joy, when thou art gone,
And I alone,
Which cannot be,
Because thou dost abide with me,
And I depend on thee;

Yet when thou dost suppresse
The cheerfulnesse
Of thy abode,
And in my powers not stirre abroad,
But leave me to my load:

O what a damp and shade
Doth me invade!
No stormie night
Can so afflict or so affright,
As thy eclipsed light

Ah Lord! do not withdraw,
Lest want of aw
Make Sinne appeare;
And when thou dost but shine lesse cleare,
Say, that thou art not here.

And then what life I have,
While Sinne doth rave,
And falsely boast,
That I may seek, but thou art lost;
Thou and alone thou know'st.

O what a deadly cold
Doth me infold!
I half beleeve,
That Sinne sayes true: but while I grieve,
Thou com'st and dost relieve.

THE ELIXER

RR

TEACH me, my God and King,
In all things thee to see,
And what I do in any thing,
To do it as for thee:

Not rudely, as a beast,
To runne into an action;
But still to make thee prepossest,
And give it his perfection.

A man that looks on glasse,
On it may stay his eye;
Or if he pleaseth, through it passe,
And then the heav'n espie.

All may of thee partake:
Nothing can be so mean,
Which with his tincture (for thy sake)
Will not grow bright and clean.

A servant with this clause
Makes drudgerie divine:
Who sweeps a room, as for thy laws,
Makes that and th' action fine.

This is the famous stone
That turneth all to gold:
For that which God doth touch and own
Cannot for lesse be told.

DEATH

A WREATH

A WREATHED garland of deserved praise,
Of praise deserved, unto thee I give,
I give to thee, who knowest all my wayes,
My crooked winding wayes, wherein I live,
Wherein I die, not live: for life is straight,
Straight as a line, and ever tends to thee,
To thee, who art more farre above deceit,
Then deceit seems above simplicitie.
Give me simplicitie, that I may live,
So live and like, that I may know thy wayes,
Know them and practise them: then shall I give
For this poore wreath, give thee a crown of praise.

DEATH

DEATH, thou wast once an uncouth hideous thing,
Nothing but bones,
The sad effect of sadder grones:
Thy mouth was open, but thou couldst not sing.

For we consider'd thee as at some six
Or ten yeares hence,
After the losse of life and sense,
Flesh being turn'd to dust, and bones to sticks.

We lookt on this side of thee, shooting short;
Where we did finde
The shells of fledge souls left behinde,
Dry dust, which sheds no tears, but may extort.

But since our Saviours death did put some bloud
Into thy face;
Thou art grown fair and full of grace,
Much in request, much sought for, as a good.

For we do now behold thee gay and glad,
As at dooms-day;
When souls shall wear their new aray,
And all thy bones with beautie shall be clad.

Therefore we can go die as sleep, and trust
Half that we have
Unto an honest faithfull grave;
Making our pillows either down, or dust.

DOOMS-DAY

Come away,
Make no delay.
Summon all the dust to rise,
Till it stirre, and rubbe the eyes;
While this member jogs the other,
Each one whispring, *Live you brother?*

Come away,
Make this the day.
Dust, alas, no musick feels,
But thy trumpet: then it kneels,
As peculiar notes and strains
Cure Tarantulaes raging pains.

Come away,
O make no stay!
Let the graves make their confession,
Lest at length they plead possession:
Fleshes stubbornnesse may have
Read that lesson to the grave.

Come away,
Thy flock doth stray.
Some to windes their bodie lend,
And in them may drown a friend:
Some in noisome vapours grow
To a plague and publick wo.

Come away,
Help our decay.
Man is out of order hurl'd,
Parcel'd out to all the world.
Lord, thy broken consort raise,
And the musick shall be praise.

JUDGEMENT

ALMIGHTIE Judge, how shall poore wretches brook
Thy dreadfull look,
Able a heart of iron to appall,
When thou shalt call
For ev'ry mans peculiar book?

What others mean to do, I know not well;
Yet I heare tell,
That some will turn thee to some leaves therein
So void of sinne,
That they in merit shall excell.

But I resolve, when thou shalt call for mine,
That to decline,
And thrust a Testament into thy hand:
Let that be scann'd.
There thou shalt finde my faults are thine.

HEAVEN

O WHO will show me those delights on high?
Echo. *I.*
Thou Echo, thou art mortall, all men know.
Echo. *No.*
Wert thou not born among the trees and leaves?
Echo. *Leaves.*
And are there any leaves, that still abide?
Echo. *Bide.*
What leaves are they? impart the matter wholly.
Echo. *Holy.*
Are holy leaves the Echo then of blisse?
Echo. *Yes.*
Then tell me, what is that supreme delight?
Echo. *Light*
Light to the minde: what shall the will enjoy?
Echo. *Joy.*
But are there cares and businesse with the pleasure?
Echo. *Leisure.*
Light, joy, and leisure; but shall they persever?
Echo. *Ever.*

LOVE

Love bade me welcome: yet my soul drew back,
Guiltie of dust and sinne.
But quick-ey'd Love, observing me grow slack
From my first entrance in,
Drew nearer to me, sweetly questioning,
If I lack'd any thing.

A guest, I answer'd, worthy to be here:
Love said, you shall be he.
I the unkinde, ungratefull? Ah my deare,
I cannot look on thee.
Love took my hand, and smiling did reply,
Who made the eyes but I?

Truth Lord, but I have marr'd them: let my shame
Go where it doth deserve.
And know you not, sayes Love, who bore the blame?
My deare, then I will serve.
You must sit down, sayes Love, and taste my meat:
So I did sit and eat.

FINIS

Glorie be to God on high, and on earth peace, good will towards men.

THE CHURCH MILITANT

ALMIGHTIE Lord, who from thy glorious throne
Seest and rulest all things ev'n as one:
The smallest ant or atome knows thy power,
Known also to each minute of an houre:
Much more do Common-weals acknowledge thee,
And wrap their policies in thy decree,
Complying with thy counsels, doing nought
Which doth not meet with an eternall thought.
But above all, thy Church and Spouse doth prove
Not the decrees of power, but bands of love.
Early didst thou arise to plant this vine,
Which might the more indeare it to be thine.
Spices come from the East; so did thy Spouse,
Trimme as the light, sweet as the laden boughs
Of *Noahs* shadie vine, chaste as the dove;
Prepar'd and fitted to receive thy love.
The course was westward, that the sunne might light
As well our understanding as our sight,
Where th' Ark did rest, there *Abraham* began
To bring the other Ark from *Canaan*.
Moses pursu'd this: but King *Solomon*
Finish'd and fixt the old religion.
When it grew loose, the Jews did hope in vain
By nailing Christ to fasten it again.
But to the Gentiles he bore crosse and all,
Rending with earthquakes the partition-wall:

Onely whereas the Ark in glorie shone,
Now with the crosse, as with a staffe, alone,
Religion, like a pilgrime, westward bent,
Knocking at all doores, ever as she went.
Yet as the sunne, though forward be his flight,
Listens behinde him, and allows some light,
Till all depart: so went the Church her way,
Letting, while one foot stept, the other stay
Among the eastern nations for a time,
Till both removed to the western clime.
To *Egypt* first she came, where they did prove
Wonders of anger once, but now of love.
The ten Commandments there did flourish more
Then the ten bitter plagues had done before.
Holy *Macarius* and great *Anthonie*
Made *Pharaoh Moses*, changing th' historie.
Goshen was darknesse, *Egypt* full of lights,
Nilus for monsters brought forth Israelites.
Such power hath mightie Baptisme to produce
For things misshapen, things of highest use.
How deare to me, O God, thy counsels are!
Who may with thee compare?
Religion thence fled into *Greece*, where arts
Gave her the highest place in all mens hearts.
Learning was pos'd, Philosophie was set,
Sophisters taken in a fishers net.
Plato and *Aristotle* were at a losse,
And wheel'd about again to spell *Christ-Crosse*.
Prayers chas'd syllogismes into their den,
And *Ergo* was transform'd into *Amen*.
Though *Greece* took horse as soon as *Egypt* did,
And *Rome* as both; yet *Egypt* faster rid,
And spent her period and prefixed time
Before the other. *Greece* being past her prime,

Religion went to *Rome*, subduing those,
Who, that they might subdue, made all their foes.
The Warrier his deere'skarres no more resounds,
But seems to yeeld Christ hath the greater wounds,
Wounds willingly endur'd to work his blisse,
Who by an ambush lost his Paradise.
The great heart stoops, and taketh from the dust
A sad repentance, not the spoils of lust:
Quitting his spear, lest it should pierce again
Him in his members, who for him was slain.
The Shepherds hook grew to a scepter here,
Giving new names and numbers to the yeare.
But th' Empire dwelt in *Greece*, to comfort them
Who were cut short in *Alexanders* stemme.
In both of these Prowesse and Arts did tame
And tune mens hearts against the Gospel came.
Which using, and not fearing skill in th' one,
Or strength in th' other, did erect her throne.
Many a rent and struggling th' Empire knew,
(As dying things are wont) untill it flew
At length to *Germanie*, still westward bending,
And there the Churches festivall attending:
That as before Empire and Arts made way,
(For no lesse Harbingers would serve then they)
So they might still, and point us out the place [face.
Where first the Church should raise her down-cast
Strength levels grounds, Art makes a garden there;
Then showres Religion, and makes all to bear.
Spain in the Empire shar'd with *Germanie*,
But *England* in the higher victorie:
Giving the Church a crown to keep her state,
And not go lesse then she had done of late.
Constantines British line meant this of old,
And did this mysterie wrap up and fold

Within a sheet of paper, which was rent
From times great Chronicle, and hither sent.
Thus both the Church and Sunne together ran
Unto the farthest old meridian.
How deare to me, O God, thy counsels are!
Who may with thee compare?
Much about one and the same time and place,
Both where and when the Church began her race,
Sinne did set out of Eastern *Babylon*,
And travell'd westward also: journeying on
He chid the Church away, where e're he came,
Breaking her peace, and tainting her good name.
At first he got to *Egypt*, and did sow
Gardens of gods, which ev'ry yeare did grow,
Fresh and fine deities. They were at great cost,
Who for a god clearely a sallet lost.
Ah, what a thing is man devoid of grace,
Adoring garlick with an humble face,
Begging his food of that which he may eat,
Starving the while he worshippeth his meat!
Who makes a root his god, how low is he,
If God and man be sever'd infinitely!
What wretchednesse can give him any room,
Whose house is foul, while he adores his broom?
None will beleeve this now, though money be
In us the same transplanted foolerie.
Thus Sinne in *Egypt* sneaked for a while;
His highest was an ox or crocodile,
And such poore game. Thence he to *Greece* doth [passe,
And being craftier much then Goodnesse was,
He left behinde him garrisons of sinnes
To make good that which ev'ry day he winnes.
Here Sinne took heart, and for a garden-bed
Rich shrines and oracles he purchased:

He grew a gallant, and would needs foretell
As well what should befall, as what befell.
Nay, he became a poet, and would serve
His pills of sublimate in that conserve.
The world came both with hands and purses full
To this great lotterie, and all would pull.
But all was glorious cheating, brave deceit,
Where some poore truths were shuffled for a bait
To credit him, and to discredit those
Who after him should braver truths disclose.
From *Greece* he went to *Rome:* and as before
He was a God, now he's an Emperour.
Nero and others lodg'd him bravely there,
Put him in trust to rule the Romane sphere.
Glorie was his chief instrument of old:
Pleasure succeeded straight, when that grew cold.
Which soon was blown to such a mightie flame,
That though our Saviour did destroy the game,
Disparking oracles, and all their treasure,
Setting affliction to encounter pleasure;
Yet did a rogue with hope of carnall joy
Cheat the most subtill nations. Who so coy,
So trimme, as *Greece* and *Egypt?* yet their hearts
Are given over, for their curious arts,
To such Mahometan stupidities,
As the old heathen would deem prodigies.
How deare to me, O God, thy counsels are!
Who may with thee compare?
Onely the West and *Rome* do keep them free
From this contagious infidelitie.
And this is all the Rock, whereof they boast,
As *Rome* will one day finde unto her cost.
Sinne being not able to extirpate quite
The Churches here, bravely resolv'd one night

To be a Church-man too, and wear a Mitre :
The old debauched ruffian would turn writer.
I saw him in his studie, where he sate
Busie in controversies sprung of late.
A gown and pen became him wondrous well :
His grave aspect had more of heav'n then hell :
Onely there was a handsome picture by,
To which he lent a corner of his eye.
As Sinne in *Greece* a Prophet was before,
And in old *Rome* a mightie Emperour ;
So now being Priest he plainly did professe
To make a jest of Christs three offices :
The rather since his scatter'd jugglings were
United now in one both time and sphere.
From *Egypt* he took pettie deities,
From *Greece* oracular infallibilities,
And from old *Rome* the libertie of pleasure,
By free dispensings of the Churches treasure.
Then in memoriall of his ancient throne
He did surname his palace, *Babylon*.
Yet that he might the better gain all nations,
And make that name good by their transmigrations ;
From all these places, but at divers times,
He took fine vizards to conceal his crimes :
From *Egypt* Anchorisme and retirednesse,
Learning from *Greece*, from old *Rome* statelinesse :
And blending these he carri'd all mens eyes,
While Truth sat by, counting his victories :
Whereby he grew apace and scorn'd to use
Such force as once did captivate the Jews ;
But did bewitch, and finely work each nation
Into a voluntarie transmigration.
All poste to *Rome :* Princes submit their necks
Either t' his publick foot or private tricks.

It did not fit his gravitie to stirre,
Nor his long journey, nor his gout and furre.
Therefore he sent out able ministers,
Statesmen within, without doores cloisterers:
Who without spear, or sword, or other drumme
Then what was in their tongue, did overcome;
And having conquer'd, did so strangely rule,
That the whole world did seem but the Popes mule.
As new and old *Rome* did one Empire twist;
So both together are one Antichrist,
Yet with two faces, as their *Janus* was;
Being in this their old crackt looking-glasse.
How deare to me, O God, thy counsels are!
Who may with thee compare?
Thus Sinne triumphs in Western *Babylon;*
Yet not as Sinne, but as Religion.
Of his two thrones he made the latter best,
And to defray his journey from the east.
Old and new *Babylon* are to hell and night,
As is the moon and sunne to heav'n and light.
When th' one did set, the other did take place,
Confronting equally the law and grace.
They are hells land-marks, Satans double crest:
They are Sinnes nipples, feeding th' east and west.
But as in vice the copie still exceeds
The pattern, but not so in vertuous deeds;
So though Sinne made his latter seat the better,
The latter Church is to the first a debter.
The second Temple could not reach the first:
And the late reformation never durst
Compare with ancient times and purer yeares;
But in the Jews and us deserveth tears.
Nay, it shall ev'ry yeare decrease and fade;
Till such a darknesse do the world invade

At Christs last coming, as his first did finde:
Yet must there such proportions be assign'd
To these diminishings, as is between
The spacious world and *Jurie* to be seen.
Religion stands on tip-toe in our land,
Readie to passe to the *American* strand.
When height of malice, and prodigious lusts,
Impudent sinning, witchcrafts, and distrusts
(The marks of future bane) shall fill our cup
Unto the brimme, and make our measure up;
When *Sein* shall swallow *Tiber*, and the *Thames*
By letting in them both, pollutes her streams:
When *Italie* of us shall have her will,
And all her calender of sinnes fulfill;
Whereby one may fortell, what sinnes next yeare
Shall both in *France* and *England* domineer:
Then shall Religion to *America* flee:
They have their times of Gospel, ev'n as we.
My God, thou dost prepare for them a way
By carrying first their gold from them away:
For gold and grace did never yet agree:
Religion alwaies sides with povertie.
We think we rob them, but we think amisse:
We are more poore, and they more rich by this.
Thou wilt revenge their quarrell, making grace
To pay our debts, and leave our ancient place
To go to them, while that which now their nation
But lends to us, shall be our desolation.
Yet as the Church shall thither westward flie,
So Sinne shall trace and dog her instantly:
They have their period also and set times
Both for their vertuous actions and their crimes.
And where of old the Empire and the Arts
Usher'd the Gospel ever in mens hearts,

Spain hath done one ; when Arts perform the other,
The Church shall come, & Sinne the Church shall smother :
That when they haue accomplished the round,
And met in th' east their first and ancient sound,
Judgement may meet them both & search them round.
Thus do both lights, as well in Church as Sunne,
Light one another, and together runne.
Thus also Sinne and Darknesse follow still
The Church and Sunne with all their power and skill.
But as the Sunne still goes both west and east ;
So also did the Church by going west
Still eastward go ; because it drew more neare
To time and place, where judgement shall appeare.
How deare to me, O God, thy counsels are !
Who may with thee compare ?

L'ENVOY

King of glorie, King of peace,
With the one make warre to cease;
With the other blesse thy sheep,
Thee to love, in thee to sleep.
Let not Sinne devoure thy fold,
Bragging that thy bloud is cold,
That thy death is also dead,
While his conquests dayly spread;
That thy flesh hath lost his food,
And thy Crosse is common wood.
Choke him, let him say no more,
But reserve his breath in store,
Till thy conquests and his fall
Make his sighs to use it all,
And then bargain with the winde
To discharge what is behinde.

Blessed be God alone,
Thrice blessed Three in One.

FINIS

THE TITLES OF THE SEVERALL POEMS CONTAINED IN THIS BOOK

INDEX

INDEX

FINIS

A PRIEST
To the
TEMPLE,

OR

The Countrey Parson

His

CHARACTER,

And

Rule of Holy Life.

The Authour,

Mr. G. H.

THE AUTHOUR TO THE READER

Being desirous, thorow the mercy of God, to please Him, for Whom I am and live, and Who giveth mee my desires and performances; and considering with myself that the way to please Him is to feed my flocke diligently and faithfully, since our Saviour hath made that the argument of a pastour's love, I have resolved to set down the form and character of a true pastour, that I may have a mark to aim at; which also I will set as high as I can, since hee shoots higher that threatens the moon, than he that aims at a tree. Not that I think if a man do not all which is here expressed hee presently sinns, and displeases God, but that it is a good strife to go as farre as we can in pleasing of Him, Who hath done so much for us. The Lord prosper the intention to myselfe, and others who may not despise my poor labours, but add to those points which I have observed, untill the book grow to a compleat pastorall.

GEO. HERBERT.

1632.

CONTENTS

CONTENTS

A Priest to the Temple

CHAP. I

Of a Pastor

A PASTOR is the deputy of Christ for the reducing of man to the obedience of God. This definition is evident, and containes the direct steps of pastorall duty and auctority. For, first, man fell from God by disobedience. Secondly, Christ is the glorious instrument of God for the revoking of man. Thirdly, Christ being not to continue on earth, but after Hee had fulfilled the work of reconciliation to be received up into heaven, He constituted deputies in His place; and these are priests. And therefore St. Paul, in the beginning of his Epistles, professeth this; and in the first to the Colossians plainly avoucheth that he 'fils up that which is behinde of the afflictions of Christ in his flesh, for His Bodie's sake, which is the Church.' Wherein is contained the complete definition of a minister. Out of this chartre of the priesthood may be plainly gathered both the dignity thereof and the duty: the dignity, in that a priest may do that which Christ did, and by His auctority and as His vicegerent; the duty, in that a priest is to do that which Christ did, and after His manner, both for doctrine and life.

CHAP. II

Their Diversities

Of pastors (intending mine own nation only, and also therein setting aside the reverend prelates of the Church, to whom this discourse ariseth not), some live in the universities, some in noble houses, some in parishes, residing on their cures. Of those that live in the universities, some live there in office, whose rule is that of the Apostle (Romans xii. 6): 'Having gifts differing according to the grace that is given to us, whether prophecy, let us prophecy according to the proportion of faith; or ministry, let us wait on our ministering; or he that teacheth, on teaching,' &c.; 'he that ruleth, let him do it with diligence,' &c. Some in a preparatory way, whose aim and labour must be not only to get knowledge, but to subdue and mortifie all lusts and affections; and not to think that when they have read the Fathers or Schoolmen, a minister is made and the thing done. The greatest and hardest preparation is within; for 'Unto the ungodly saith God, Why dost thou preach My laws, and takest My covenant in thy mouth?' (Ps. l. 16.) Those that live in noble houses are called chaplains, whose duty and obligation being the same to the houses they live in, as a parson's to his parish, in describing the one (which is indeed the bent of my discourse) the other will be manifest. Let not chaplains think themselves so free, as many of them do, and because they have different names, think their office different. Doubtlesse they are parsons of the families they live in, and are entertained to that end, either by an open or implicit covenant. Before they are in orders, they may be received for companions or discoursers; but after a man is once minister, he cannot agree to come into any house, where he shall not exercise what he is, unlesse he forsake his plough and look back (St. Luke ix. 62). Wherefore they are not to be over-submissive and base, but to keep up with the lord and lady of the house, and to preserve a boldness with them and all, even so far as reproof to their very face, when occasion cals, but seasonably and discreetly. They who do not thus, while they remember their earthly lord, do much forget their heavenly; they wrong the priesthood, neglect their duty, and shall be so farre from that which they seek with their over-submissiveness and cringings, that they shall ever be despised. They who for the hope of promotion neglect any necessary admonition or reproof, sell (with Judas) their Lord and Master.

CHAP. III

The Parson's Life

THE countrey parson is exceeding exact in his life, being holy, just, prudent, temperate, bold, grave, in all his wayes. And because the two highest points of life wherein a Christian is most seen are patience and mortification—patience in regard of afflictions; mortification in regard of lusts and affections, and the stupifying and deadening of all the clamarous powers of the soul—therefore he hath thoroughly studied these, that he may be an absolute master and commander of himself for all the purposes which God hath ordained him. Yet in these points he labours most in those things which are most apt to scandalize his parish. And first, because countrey people live hardly, and therefore as feeling their own sweat, and consequently knowing the price of mony, are offended much with any who by hard usage increase their travell, the countrey parson is very circumspect in avoiding all covetousnesse, neither being greedy to get, nor niggardly to keep, nor troubled to lose any worldly wealth; but in all his words and actions slighting and disesteeming it, even to a wondring that the world should so much value wealth, which in the day of wrath hath not one dramme of comfort for us. Secondly, because luxury is a very visible sin, the parson is very careful to avoid all the kinds thereof; but especially that of drinking, because it is the most popular vice; into which, if he come, he prostitutes himself both to shame and sin, and, by having 'fellowship with the unfruitfull works of darknesse' [Ephesians v. 11] he disableth himself of authority to reprove them; for sins make all equall whom they finde together, and then they are worst who ought to be best. Neither is it for the servant of Christ to haunt innes, or tavernes or alehouses, to the dishonour of his person and office. The parson doth not so, but orders his life in such a fashion, that when death takes him, as the Jewes and Judas did Christ, he may say as He did, 'I sate daily with you teaching in the Temple' [St. Matthew xxvi. 55]. Thirdly, because countrey people (as indeed all honest men) do much esteem their word, it being the life of buying and selling and dealing in the world; therefore the parson is very strict in keeping his word, though it be to his own hindrance, as knowing that if he be not so he wil quickly be discovered and disregarded: neither will they beleeve him in the pulpit whom they cannot trust in his conversation. As for oaths and apparell, the disorders thereof are also very manifest. The parson's yea is *yea*, and nay, *nay*; and his apparell plaine, but reverend and clean, without spots or dust or smell; the purity of his mind breaking out and dilating itselfe even to his body, cloaths, and habitation.

CHAP. IV

The Parson's Knowledg

THE countrey parson is full of all knowledg. They say it is an ill mason that refuseth any stone; and there is no knowledg, but in a skilfull hand, serves either positively as it is, or else to illustrate some other knowledge. He condescends even to the knowledge of tillage and pastorage, and makes great use of them in teaching, because people, by what they understand, are best led to what they understand not. But the chief and top of his knowledge consists in the book of books, the storehouse and magazene of life and comfort, the Holy Scriptures. There he sucks and lives. In the Scriptures hee finds four things: precepts for life, doctrines for knowledge, examples for illustration, and promises for comfort. These he hath digested severally. But for the understanding of these, the means he useth are first, a holy life, remembring what his Master saith, that 'if any do God's will, he shall know of the doctrine' (John vii. [17]); and assuring himself that wicked men, however learned, do not know the Scriptures, because they feel them not, and because they are not understood but with the same Spirit that writ them. The second means is prayer, which if it be necessary even in temporall things, how much more in things of another world, where the well is deep, and we have nothing of ourselves to draw with? Wherefore he ever begins the reading of the Scripture with some short inward ejaculation, as, 'Lord, open mine eyes, that I may see the wondrous things of Thy law,' &c. [Ps. cxix. 18]. The third means is a diligent collation of Scripture with Scripture. For all truth being consonant to itself, and all being penn'd by one and the self-same

Spirit, it cannot be but that an industrious and judicious comparing of place with place must be a singular help for the right understanding of the Scriptures. To this may be added the consideration of any text with the coherence thereof, touching what goes before and what follows after, as also the scope of the Holy Ghost. When the Apostles would have called down fire from heaven, they were reproved, as ignorant of what spirit they were. For the law required one thing, and the gospel another; yet as diverse, not as repugnant; therefore the spirit of both is to be considered and weighed. The fourth means are Commenters and Fathers who have handled the places controverted, which the parson by no means refuseth. As he doth not so study others as to neglect the grace of God in himself, and what the Holy Spirit teacheth him, so doth he assure himself that God in all ages hath had His servants, to whom He hath revealed His truth as well as to him; and that as one countrey doth not bear all things, that there may be a commerce, so neither hath God opened, or will open, all to one, that there may be a traffick in knowledg between the servants of God, for the planting both of love and humility. Wherefore he hath one comment at least upon every book of Scripture; and ploughing with this and his own meditations, he enters into the secrets of God treasured in the Holy Scripture.

CHAP. V

The Parson's accessory Knowledges

THE countrey parson hath read the Fathers also, and the Schoolmen, and the later writers, or a good proportion of all, out of all which he hath compiled a book and body of divinity, which is the storehouse of his sermons, and which he preacheth all his life, but diversely clothed, illustrated, and inlarged. For though the world is full of such composures, yet every man's own is fittest, readiest, and most savoury to him. Besides, this being to be done in his younger and preparatory times, it is an honest joy ever after to looke upon his well-spent hours. This body he made by way of expounding the Church Catechisme, to which all divinity may easily be reduced; for it being indifferent in itselfe to choose any method, that is best to be chosen, of which there is likelyest to be most use. Now catechising being a work of singular and admirable benefit to the Church of God, and a thing required under canonicall obedience, the expounding of our Catechisme must needs be the most usefull forme. Yet hath the parson, besides this laborious work, a slighter forme of catechising, fitter for country people; according as his audience is, so he useth one or other, or sometimes both, if his audience be intermixed. He greatly esteemes also of cases of conscience, wherein he is much versed. And, indeed, herein is the greatest ability of a parson, to lead his people exactly in the wayes of truth, so that they neither decline to the right hand nor to the left. Neither let any think this a slight thing. For every one hath not digested when it is a sin to take something for mony lent, or when not; when it is a fault to discover another's fault, or when not; when the affections of the soul in desiring and procuring increase of means or honour be a sin of covetousness or ambition, and when not; when the appetites of the body in eating, drinking, sleep, and the pleasure that comes with sleep, be sins of gluttony, drunkenness, sloath, lust, and when not; and so in many circumstances of actions. Now if a shepherd know not which grass will bane, or which not, how is he fit to be a shepherd?

Wherefore the parson hath thoroughly canvassed al the particulars of humane actions, at least all those which he observeth are most incident to his parish.

CHAP. VI

The Parson Praying

The countrey parson, when he is to read divine services, composeth himselfe to all possible reverence, lifting up his heart and hands and eyes, and using all other gestures which may expresse a hearty and unfeyned devotion. This he doth, first, as being truly touched and amazed with the majesty of God, before Whom he then presents himself; yet not as himself alone, but as presenting with himself the whole congregation, whose sins he then beares, and brings with his own to the heavenly altar to be bathed and washed in the sacred laver of Christ's blood. Secondly, as this is the true reason of his inward feare, so he is content to expresse this outwardly to the utmost of his power; that, being first affected himself, hee may affect also his people, knowing that no sermon moves them so much to a reverence, which they forget againe, when they come to pray, as a devout behaviour in the very act of praying. Accordingly his voyce is humble, his words treatable and slow, yet not so slow neither as to let the fervency of the supplicant hang and dy between speaking; but with a grave livelinesse, between fear and zeal, pausing yet pressing, he performes his duty. Besides his example, he having often instructed his people how to carry themselves in divine service, exacts of them all possible reverence, by no means enduring either talking, or sleeping, or gazing, or leaning, or halfe-kneeling, or any undutifull behaviour in them; but causing them, when they sit, or stand, or kneel, to do all in a strait and steady posture, as attending to what is done in the church, and every one, man and child, answering aloud both Amen, and all other answers which are on the clerk's and people's part to answer; which answers also are to be done not in a hudling or slubbering fashion, gaping, or scratching the head, or spitting even, in the midst of their answer, but gently and pausably, thinking what they say; so that while they answer, 'As it was in the beginning,' &c., they meditate as they speak, that God hath ever had His people, that have glorified Him as wel as now, and that He shall have so for ever: and the like in other answers. This is that which the Apostle cals a reasonable service (Romans xii. [1]), when we speak not as parrats, without reason, or offer up such sacrifices as they did of old, which was of beasts devoyd of reason; but when we use our reason and apply our powers to the service of Him that gives them. If there be any of the gentry or nobility of the parish who sometimes make it a piece of state not to come at the beginning of service with their poor neighbours, but at mid-prayers, both to their own loss and of theirs also who gaze upon them when they come in, and neglect the present service of God, he by no means suffers it, but after divers gentle admonitions, if they persevere, he causes them to be presented; or if the poor churchwardens be affrighted with their greatness, notwithstanding his instruction that they ought not to be so, but even to let the world sinke, so they do their duty, he presents them himself, only protesting to them that not any ill-will draws him to it, but the debt and obligation of his calling, being to obey God rather than men.

CHAP. VII

The Parson Preaching

The countrey parson preacheth constantly; the pulpit is his joy and his throne: if he at any time intermit, it is either for want of health, or against some great festivall, that he may the better celebrate it, or for the variety of the hearers, that he may be heard at his returne more attentively. When he intermits, he is ever very well supplyed by some able man, who treads in his steps, and will not throw down what he hath built; whom also he entreats to press some point that he himself hath often urged with no great success, that so, 'in the mouth of two or three witnesses' [St. Matthew xviii. 16] the truth may be more established. When he preacheth, he procures attention by all possible art; both by earnestnesse of speech—it being naturall to men to think, that where is much earnestness, there is somewhat worth hearing—and by a diligent and busy cast of his eye on his auditors, with letting them know that he observes who marks, and who not; and with particularizing of his speech now to the younger sort, then to the elder, now to the poor, and now to the rich—'This is for you, and this is for you;' for particulars ever touch and awake more then generalls. Herein also he serves himselfe of the judgements of God, as of those of ancient times, so especially of the late ones, and those most which are nearest to his parish; for people are very attentive at such discourses, and think it behoves them to be so when God is so neer them, and even over their heads. Sometimes he tells them stories and sayings of others, according as his text invites him; for them also men heed, and remember better then exhortations; which, though earnest, yet often dy with the sermon, especially with countrey people, which are thick, and heavy, and hard to raise to a point of zeal and fervency, and need a mountaine of fire to kindle them; but stories and sayings they will well remember. He often tels them that sermons are dangerous things; that none goes out of church as he came in, but either better or worse; that none is careless before his judg, and that the Word of God shal judge us. By these and other means the parson procures attention; but the character of his sermon is holiness; he is not witty, or learned, or eloquent, but holy—a character that Hermogenes never dream'd of, and therefore he could give no precepts thereof. But it is gained, first, by choosing texts of devotion, not controversy, moving and ravishing texts, whereof the Scriptures are full. Secondly, by dipping and seasoning all our words and sentences in our hearts before they come into our mouths, truly affecting and cordially expressing all that we say; so that the auditors may plainly perceive that every word is hart-deep. Thirdly, by turning often, and making many apostrophes to God,—as, 'O Lord, blesse my people, and teach them this point;' or, 'O my Master, on Whose errand I come, let me hold my peace, and do Thou speak Thyselfe; for Thou art love, and when Thou teachest, all are scholers.' Some such irradiations scatteringly in the sermon carry great holiness in them. The Prophets are admirable in this. So Isaiah lxvi. [1]: 'Oh that Thou wouldst rend the heavens, that Thou wouldst come down,' &c. And Jeremy (chapt. x. [23]), after he had complained of the desolation of Israel, turnes to God suddenly, 'Oh Lord, I know that the way of man is not in himself,' &c. Fourthly, by frequent wishes of the people's good, and joying therein, though he himself were, with St. Paul, even sacrificed upon the service of their faith. For there is no greater sign of holinesse than the procuring and rejoycing in another's good. And herein St. Paul excelled in all his epistles. How did he put the Romans in all his prayers! (Rom. i. 9). And ceased not to give thanks for the Ephesians (Eph. i. 16); and for the Corinthians (I. chap. i. 4). And for the Philippians made request with joy (chap. i. 4). And is in contention for them whether to live or dy, be with them or Christ (verse 23); which, setting aside his care of his flock, were a madnesse to doubt of. What an admirable epistle is the second to the Corinthians! how full of affections! He joyes and he is sorry, he grieves and he gloryes; never was there such care of a flock expressed, save in the great Shepherd of the fold, Who first shed tears over Jerusalem, and afterwards blood. Therefore this care may be learn'd there, and then woven into sermons, which will make them appear exceeding reverend and holy. Lastly, by an often urging of the presence and majesty of God, by these or such like speeches: 'Oh let us all take heed what we do! God sees us; He sees whether I speak as I ought, or you hear as you ought; He sees hearts as we see faces: He is among us; for if we be here, Hee must be here, since we are here by Him, and without Him could not be here.' Then turning the discourse to his majesty, 'And He is a great God and terrible, as great in mercy, so great in judgement. There are but two devouring elements, fire and water; He hath both in Him; His voyce is "as the sound of many waters" (Revelation i. [15]); and He Himselfe "is a consuming fire"' (Hebrews xii. [29]). Such discourses show very holy. The parson's method in handling of a text consists of two parts: first, a plain and evident declaration of the meaning of the text; and secondly, some choyce observations drawn out of the whole text, as it lyes entire and unbroken in the Scripture itself. This he thinks naturall, and sweet, and grave. Whereas the other way, of crumbling a text into small parts, as the person speaking or spoken to, the subject and object, and the like, hath neither in it sweetnesse, nor gravity, nor variety; since the words apart are not Scripture, but a dictionary, and may be considered alike in all the Scripture. The parson exceeds not an hour in preaching, because all ages have thought that a competency; and he that profits not in that time will lesse afterwards, the same affection which made him not profit before making him then weary; and so he grows from not relishing to loathing.

CHAP. VIII

The Parson on Sundays

THE countrey parson, as soon as he awakes on Sunday morning, presently falls to work, and seems to himselfe so as a market-man is when the market-day comes, or a shopkeeper when customers use to come in. His thoughts are full of making the best of the day, and contriving it to his best gaines. To this end, besides his ordinary prayers, he makes a peculiar one for a blessing on the exercises of the day; that nothing befall him unworthy of that Majesty before which he is to present himself, but that all may be done with reverence to His glory, and with edification to his flock; humbly beseeching his Master, that how or whenever He punish him, it be not in his ministry. Then he turns to request for his people that the Lord would be pleased to sanctifie them all, that they may come with holy hearts and awful minds into the congregation, and that the good God would pardon all those who come with lesse prepared hearts then they ought. This done, he sets himself to the consideration of the duties of the day; and if there be any extraordinary addition to the customary exercises, either from the time of the year, or from the State, or from God, by a child born or dead, or any other accident, he contrives how and in what manner to induce it to the best advantage. Afterwards, when the hour calls, with his family attending him, he goes to church, at his first entrance humbly adoring and worshipping the invisible majesty and presence of Almighty God, and blessing the people, either openly or to himselfe. Then having read divine service twice fully, and preached in the morning, and catechized in the afternoone, he thinks he hath in some measure, according to poor and fraile man, discharged the publick duties of the congregation. The rest of the day he spends either in reconciling neighbours that are at variance, or in visiting the sick, or in exhortations to some of his flock by themselves, whom his sermons cannot or do not reach. And every one is more awaked, when we come and say, 'Thou art the man' [2 Samuel xii. 7]. This way he findes exceeding usefull and winning; and these exhortations he cals his privy purse, even as princes have theirs besides their publick disbursements. At night he thinks it a very fit time, both sutable to the joy of the day and without hindrance to publick duties, either to entertaine some of his neighbours or to be entertained of them; where he takes occasion to discourse of such things as are both profitable and pleasant, and to raise up their mindes to apprehend God's good blessing to our Church and State; that order is kept in the one, and peace in the other, without disturbance, or interruption of publick divine offices. As he opened the day with prayer, so he closeth it, humbly beseeching the Almighty to pardon and accept our poor services, and to improve them, that we may grow therein, and that our feet may be like hindes' feet, ever climbing up higher and higher unto Him.

CHAP. IX

The Parson's State of Life

THE countrey parson considering that virginity is a higher state than matrimony, and that the ministry requires the best and highest things, is rather unmarryed, than marryed. But yet as the temper of his body may be, or as the temper of his parish may be, where he may have occasion to converse with women, and that among suspicious men, and other like circumstances considered, he is rather married than unmarried. Let him communicate the thing often by prayer unto God, and as His grace shall direct him, so let him proceed. If he be unmarried and keepe house, he hath not a woman in his house, but finds opportunities of having his meat dress'd, and other services done, by men-servants at home, and his linnen washed abroad. If he be unmarryed, and sojourne, he never talkes with any woman alone, but in the audience of others; and that seldom, and then also in a serious manner, never jestingly or sportfully. He is very circumspect in all companyes, both of his behaviour, speech, and very looks, knowing himself to be both suspected and envyed. If he stand steadfast in his heart, having no necessity, but hath power over his own will, and hath so decreed in his heart that he will keep himself a virgin, he spends his dayes in fasting and prayer, and blesseth God for the gift of continency, knowing that it can no way be preserved but only by those means by which at first it was obtained. He therefore thinkes it not enough for him to observe the fasting dayes of the Church, and the dayly prayers enjoyned him by auctority, which he observeth out of humble conformity and obedience, but adds to them, out of choyce and devotion, some other dayes for fasting and hours for prayers; and by these hee keeps his body tame, serviceable, and healthfull, and his soul fervent, active, young, and lusty as an eagle. He often readeth the lives of the primitive monks, hermits, and virgins, and wondreth not so much at their patient suffering, and cheerfull dying, under persecuting emperours (though that, indeed, be very admirable), as at their daily temperance, abstinence, watchings, and constant prayers and mortifications in the times of peace and prosperity. To put on the profound humility and the exact temperance of our Lord Jesus, with other exemplary vertues of that sort, and to keep them on in the sunshine and noone of prosperity, he findeth to be as necessary, and as difficult at least, as to be cloathed with perfect patience and Christian fortitude in the cold midnight stormes of persecution and adversity. He keepeth his watch and ward night and day against the proper and peculiar temptations of his state of life, which are principally these two—spirituall pride, and impurity of heart; against these ghostly enemies he girdeth up his loynes, keepes the imagination from roving, puts on the whole armour of God, and by the vertue of the shield of faith he is not afraid of the pestilence that walketh in darknesse (carnall impurity), nor of the sicknesse that destroyeth at noone-day (ghostly pride and self-conceite). Other temptations he hath, which, like mortall enemies, may sometimes disquiet him likewise; for the humane soul, being bounded and kept in her sensitive faculty, will runne out more or less in her intellectuall. Originall concupiscence is such an active thing, by reason of continuall inward or outward temptations, that it is ever attempting or doing one mischief or other; ambition, or untimely desire of promotion to an higher state or place, under colour of accommodation or necessary provision, is a common temptation to men of any eminency, especially being single men; curiosity in prying into high speculative and unprofitable questions is another great stumbling-block to the holinesse of scholers. These and many other 'spiritual wickednesses in high places' [Ephes. vi. 12] doth the parson fear, or experiment, or both; and that much more being single then if he were married; for then commonly the stream of temptations is turned another way—into covetousnesse, love of pleasure or ease, or the like. If the parson be unmarryed, and means to continue so, he doth at least as much as hath been said. If he be marryed, the choyce of his wife was made rather by his eare then by his eye; his judgement, not his affection, found out a fit wife for him, whose humble and liberall disposition he preferred before beauty, riches, or honour. He knew that (the good instrument of God to bring women to heaven) a wise and loving husband could, out of humility, produce any speciall grace of faith, patience, meeknesse, love, obedience, &c., and out of liberality make her fruitfull in all good works. As hee is just in all things, so is he to his wife also, counting nothing so much his owne as that he may be unjust unto it. Therefore he gives her respect both afore her servants and others, and halfe at least of the government of the house, reserving so much of the affaires as serve for a diversion for him; yet never so giving over the raines but that he sometimes looks how things go, demanding an account, but not by the way of an account. And this must bee done the oftner or the seldomer, according as hee is satisfied of his wife's discretion.

CHAP. X

The Parson in his House

The parson is very exact in the governing of his house, making it a copy and modell for his parish. He knows the temper and pulse of every person in his house, and accordingly either meets with their vices or advanceth their vertues. His wife is either religious, or night and day he is winning her to it. Instead of the qualities of the world, he requires onely three of her: first, a trayning up of her children and mayds in the fear of God, with prayers, and catechizing, and all religious duties. Secondly, a curing and healing of all wounds and sores with her owne hands; which skill either she brought with her, or he takes care she shall learn it of some religious neighbour. Thirdly, a providing for her family in such sort as that neither they want a competent sustentation, nor her husband be brought in debt. His children he first makes Christians, and then Commonwealth's men; the one he owes to his heavenly countrey, the other to his earthly, having no title to either except he do good to both. Therefore, having seasoned them with all piety, not only of words, in praying and reading, but in actions, in visiting other sick children and tending their wounds, and sending his charity by them to the poor, and somtimes giving them a little money to do it of themselves, that they get a delight in it, and enter favour with God, Who weighs even children's actions (I. Kings xiv. 12, 13). He afterwards turnes his care to fit all their dispositions with some calling, not sparing the eldest, but giving him the prerogative of his father's profession, which happily for his other children he is not able to do. Yet in binding them prentices (in case he think fit to do so) he takes care not to put them into vain trades and unbefitting the reverence of their father's calling, such as are tavernes for men, and lace-making for women; because those trades, for the most part, serve but the vices and vanities of the world, which he is to deny and not augment. However, he resolves with himself never to omit any present good deed of charity, in consideration of providing a stock for his children; but assures himselfe that mony thus lent to God is placed surer for his children's advantage than if it were given to the Chamber of London. Good deeds and good breeding are his two great stocks for his children: if God give anything above those, and not spent in them, he blesseth God, and lays it out as he sees cause. His servants are all religious; and were it not his duty to have them so, it were his profit; for none are so well served as by religious servants, both because they do best, and because what they do is blessed and prospers. After religion, he teacheth them that three things make a compleate servant: truth, and diligence, and neatnesse, or cleanlinesse. Those that can read are allowed times for it, and those that cannot are taught; for all in his house are either teachers or learners, or both; so that his family is a schoole of religion, and they all account that to teach the ignorant is the greatest almes. Even the wals are not idle, but something is written or painted there which may excite the reader to a thought of piety; especially the 101st Psalm, which is expressed in a fayre table, as being the rule of a family. And when they go abroad, his wife among her neighbours is the beginner of good discourses, his children among children, his servants among other servants; so that as in the house of those that are skill'd in music, all are musicians, so in the house of a preacher all are preachers. He suffers not a ly or equivocation by any means in his house, but counts it the art and secret of governing to preserve a directnesse and open plainness in all things; so that all his house knowes that there is no help for a fault done but confession. He himselfe, or his wife, takes account of sermons, and how every one profits, comparing this yeer with the last; and besides the common prayers of the family, he straitly requires of all to pray by themselves before they sleep at night and stir out in the morning, and knows what prayers they say; and, till they have learned them, makes them kneel by him, esteeming that this private praying is a more voluntary act in them then when they are called to others' prayers, and that which when they leave the family they carry with them. He keeps his servants between love and fear, according as he findes them; but generally he distributes it thus—to his children he shows more love than terrour, to his servants more terrour then love; but an old good servant boards a child. The furniture of his house is very plain, but clean, whole, and sweet, as sweet as his garden can make; for he hath no money for such things, charity being his only perfume, which deserves cost when he can spare it. His fare is plain and common, but wholesome; what he hath is little, but very good. It consisteth most of mutton, beefe, and veal. If he addes anything for a great day or a stranger, his garden or orchard supplyes it, or his barne and backside: he goes no further for any entertainment, lest he goe into the world, esteeming it absurd that he should exceed who teacheth others temperance. But those which his home produceth he refuseth not, as coming cheap and easie, and arising from the improvement of things which otherwise would be lost. Wherein he admires and imitates the wonderfull providence and thrift of the great Householder of the world; for there being two things which, as they are, are unuseful to man—the one for smallnesse, as crumbs and scattered corn and the like; the other for the foulnesse, as wash and durt, and things thereinto fallen—God hath provided creatures for both; for the first poultry, for the second swine. These save man the labour, and doing that which either he could not do, or was not fit for him to do, by taking both sorts of food into them, do as it were dress and prepare both for man in themselves, by growing themselves fit for his table. The parson in his house observes fasting dayes: and particularly as Sunday is his day of joy, so Friday his day of humiliation, which he celebrates not only with abstinence of diet, but also of company, recreation, and all outward contentments; and besides, with confession of sins and all acts of mortification. Now fasting-dayes contain a treble obligation: first, of eating lesse on that day than on other days; secondly, of eating no pleasing or over-nourishing things, as the Israelites did eate sowre herbs; thirdly, of eating no flesh, which is but the determination of the second rule by Authority to this particular. The two former obligations are much more essentiall to a true fast then the third and last; and fasting-dayes were fully performed by keeping of the two former, had not Authority interposed; so that to eat little, and that unpleasant, is the natural rule of fasting, although it be flesh. For since fasting in Scripture language is an 'afflicting of our souls' [Leviticus xvi. 29], if a peece of dry flesh at my table be more unpleasant to me then some fish there, certainly to eat the flesh and not the fish is to keep the fasting-day naturally. And it is observable that the prohibiting of flesh came from hot countryes, where both flesh alone, and much more with wine, is apt to nourish more then in cold regions, and where flesh may be much better spared and with more safety then elsewhere, where, both the people and the drink being cold and phlegmatick, the eating of flesh is an antidote to both. For it is certaine, that a weak stomack being prepossessed with flesh shall much better brooke and bear a draught of beer then if it had taken before either fish, or rootes, or such things; which will discover itself by spitting, and rheume, or flegme. To conclude: the parson, if he be in full health, keeps the three obligations, eating fish or roots, and that for quantity little, for quality unpleasant. If his body be weak and obstructed, as most students are, he cannot keep the last obligation, nor suffer others in his house that are so to keep it; but only the two former, which also in diseases of exinanition (as consumptions) must be broken; for meat was made for man, not man for meat. To all this may be added, not for emboldening the unruly, but for the comfort of the weak, that not only sicknesse breaks these obligations of fasting, but sicklinesse also; for it is as unnatural to do anything that leads me to a sicknesse to which I am inclined, as not to get out of that sicknesse, when I am in it, by any diet. One thing is evident, that an English body and a student's body are two great obstructed vessels; and there is nothing that is food and not physick, which doth lesse obstruct then flesh moderately taken; as, being immoderately taken, it is exceeding obstructive. And obstructions are the cause of most diseases.

CHAP. XI

The Parson's Courtesie

The countrey parson owing a debt of charity to the poor, and of courtesie to his other parishioners, he so distinguisheth that he keeps his money for the poor, and his table for those that are above alms. Not but that the poor are welcome also to his table, whom he sometimes purposely takes home with him, setting them close by him, and carving for them, both for his own humility and their comfort, who are much cheered with such friendlinesses. But since both is to be done, the better sort invited, and meaner relieved, he chooseth rather to give the poor money, which they can better employ to their own advantage, and suitably to their needs, then so much given in meat at dinner. Having, then, invited some of his parish, hee taketh his times to do the like to the rest; so that in the compasse of the year hee hath them all with him, because countrey people are very observant of such things, and will not be perswaded, but being not invited, they are hated. Which perswasion the parson by all means avoyds, knowing that where there are such conceits, there is no room for his doctrine to enter. Yet doth hee oftenest invite those whom hee sees take best courses, that so both they may be encouraged to persevere, and others spurred to do well, that they may enjoy the like courtesie. For though he desire that all should live well and vertuously, not for any reward of his, but for vertue's sake, yet that will not be so; and therefore, as God, although we should love Him onely for His own sake, yet out of His infinite pity hath set forth heaven for a reward to draw men to piety, and is content if at least so they will become good; so the countrey parson, who is a diligent observer and tracker of God's wayes, sets up as many encouragements to goodnesse as he can, both in honour and profit and fame, that he may, if not the best way, yet any way, make his parish good.

CHAP. XII

The Parson's Charity

The countrey parson is full of charity; it is his predominant element. For many and wonderfull things are spoken of thee, thou great vertue. To charity is given the covering of sins (I. Peter iv. 8); and the forgiveness of sins (Matthew vi. 14, Luke vii. 47); the fulfilling of the law (Romans xiii. 10); the life of faith (James ii. 26); the blessings of this life (Proverbs xxii. 9, Psalm xli. 2); and the reward of the next (Matthew xxv. 35). In brief, it is the body of religion (John xiii. 35); and the top of Christian vertues (I. Corinthians xiii. [13]). Wherefore all his works rellish of charity. When he riseth in the morning, he bethinketh himselfe what good deeds he can do that day, and presently doth them; counting that day lost wherein he hath not exercised his charity. He first considers his own parish, and takes care that there be not a begger or idle person in his parish, but that all bee in a competent way of getting their living. This he effects either by bounty, or perswasion, or by authority, making use of that excellent statute which bindes all parishes to maintaine their own. If his parish be rich, he exacts this of them; if poor, and he able, he easeth them therein. But he gives no set pension to any, for this in time will lose the name and effect of charity with the poor people, though not with God, for then they will reckon upon it as on a debt; and if it be taken away, though justly, they will murmur and repine as much as he that is disseized of his own inheritance. But the parson having a double aime, and making a hook of his charity, causeth them still to depend on him; and so by continuall and fresh bounties, unexpected to them, but resolved to himself, hee wins them to praise God more, to live more religiously, and to take more paines in their vocation, as not knowing when they shal be relieved; which otherwise they would reckon upon, and turn to idlenesse. Besides this generall provision, he hath other times of opening his hand, as at great festivals and communions, not suffering any that day that hee receives, to want a good meal suting to the joy of the occasion. But specially at hard times and dearths he even parts his living and life among them, giving some corn outright, and selling other at under-rates; and when his own stock serves not, working those that are able to the same charity, still pressing it in the pulpit and out of the pulpit, and never leaving them till he obtain his desire. Yet in all his charity he distinguisheth, giving them most who live best, and take most paines, and are most charged; so is his charity in effect a sermon. After the consideration of his own parish, he inlargeth himself, if he be able, to the neighbourhood—for that also is some kind of obligation; so doth he also to those at his door, whom God puts in his way, and makes his neighbours. But these he helps not without some testimony, except the evidence of the misery bring testimony with it. For though these testimonies also may be falsyfied, yet considering that the law allows these in case they be true, but allows by no means to give without testimony, as he obeys Authority in the one, so that being once satisfied, he allows his charity some blindnesse in the other, especially since of the two commands we are more enjoyned to be charitable then wise. But evident miseries have a naturall priviledge and exemption from all law. Whenever he gives anything, and sees them labour in thanking of him, he exacts of them to let him alone, and say rather, 'God be praised, God be glorified;' that so the thanks may go the right way, and thither onely where they are only due. So doth hee also before giving make them say their prayers first, or the creed and ten commandments, and as he finds them perfect, rewards them the more. For other givings are lay and secular, but this is to give like a priest.

CHAP. XIII

The Parson's Church

THE countrey parson hath a speciall care of his church, that all things there be decent, and befitting His name by which it is called. Therefore, first, he takes order that all things be in good repair, as walls plaistered, windows glazed, floore paved, seats whole, firm, and uniform; especially that the pulpit, and desk, and communion-table, and font be as they ought, for those great duties that are performed in them. Secondly, that the church be swept and kept clean, without dust or cobwebs, and at great festivals strawed and stuck with boughs, and perfumed with incense. Thirdly, that there be fit and proper texts of Scripture everywhere painted, and that all the painting be grave and reverend, not with light colours or foolish anticks. Fourthly, that all the books appointed by Authority be there, and those not torne or fouled, but whole and clean and well bound; and that there be a fitting and sightly communion cloth 'of fine linen, with an handsome and seemly carpet of good and costly stuffe or cloth, and all kept sweet and clean, in a strong and decent chest, with a chalice and cover, and a stoop or flagon, and a basin for almes and offerings; besides which, he hath a poor-man's box conveniently seated, to receive the charity of well-minded people, and to lay up treasure for the sick and needy.' And all this he doth, not as out of necessity, or as putting a holiness in the things, but as desiring to keep the middle way between superstition and slovenlinesse, and as following the Apostle's two great and admirable rules in things of this nature: the first whereof is, 'Let all things be done decently and in order;' the second, 'Let all things be done to edification' (I. Cor. xiv. [3]). For these two rules comprize and include the double object of our duty—God and our neighbour; the first being for the honour of God, the second for the benefit of our neighbour: so that they excellently score out the way, and fully and exactly contain, even in externall and indifferent things, what course is to be taken; and put them to great shame who deny the Scripture to be perfect.

CHAP. XIV

The Parson in Circuit

The countrey parson upon the afternoons in the week-days takes occasion sometimes to visite in person now one quarter of his parish, now another. For there he shall find his flock most naturally as they are, wallowing in the midst of their affairs; whereas on Sunday it is easie for them to compose themselves to order, which they put on as their holyday cloathes, and come to church in frame, but commonly the next day put off both. When he comes to any house, first he blesseth it, and then as hee finds the persons of the house imployed, so he formes his discourse. Those that he findes religiously imployed, he both commends them much, and furthers them when he is gone in their imployment; as, if hee findes them reading, hee furnisheth them with good books; if curing poor people, hee supplies them with receipts, and instructs them further in that skill, shewing them how acceptable such works are to God, and wishing them ever to do the cures with their own hands, and not to put them over to servants. Those that he finds busy in the works of their calling, he commendeth them also; for 'it is a good and just thing for every one to do their own busines' [I. Thess. iv. 11]. But then he admonisheth them of two things: first, that they dive not too deep into worldly affairs, plunging themselves over head and eares into carking and caring; but that they so labour as neither to labour anxiously, nor distrustfully, nor profanely. Then they labour anxiously when they overdo it, to the loss of their quiet and health; then distrustfully, when they doubt God's providence, thinking that their own labour is the cause of their thriving, as if it were in their own hands to thrive or not to thrive. Then they labour profanely, 'when they set themselves to work like brute beasts, never raising their thoughts to God, nor sanctifying their labour with daily prayer; when on the Lord's day they do unnecessary servile work, or in time of divine service on other holy days, except in the cases of extreme poverty, and in the seasons of seedtime and harvest.' Secondly, he adviseth them so to labour for wealth and maintenance as that they make not that the end of their labour, but that they may have wherewithall to serve God the better, and to do good deeds. After these discourses, if they be poor and needy whom he thus finds labouring, he gives them somewhat; and opens not only his mouth but his purse to their relief, that so they go on more cheerfully in their vocation, and himself be ever the more welcome to them. Those that the parson findes idle, or ill-employed, he chides not at first, for that were neither civill nor profitable; but always in the close, before he departs from them: yet in this he distinguisheth; for if he be a plaine countryman, he reproves him plainly, for they are not sensible of finenesse: if they be of higher quality, they commonly are quick, and sensible, and very tender of reproof; and therefore he lays his discourse so, that he comes to the point very leisurely, and oftentimes, as Nathan did, in the person of another, making them to reprove themselves. However, one way or other, he ever reproves them, that he may keep himself pure, and not be intangled in others' sinnes. Neither in this doth he forbear though there be company by; for as, when the offence is particular and against mee, I am to follow our Saviour's rule, and to take my brother aside and reprove him, so when the offence is publicke and against God, I am then to follow the Apostle's rule (I. Timothy v. 20), and to 'rebuke openly' that which is done openly. Besides these occasional discourses, the parson questions what order is kept in the house, as about prayers morning and evening, on their knees, reading of Scripture, catechizing, singing of psalms at their work and on holydays; who can read, who not; and sometimes he hears the children read himselfe, and blesseth, encouraging also the servants to learn to read, and offering to have them taught on holydays by his servants. If the parson were ashamed of particularizing in these things, he were not fit to be a parson; but he holds the rule, that nothing is little in God's service; if it once have the honour of that name, it grows great instantly. Wherefore neither disdaineth he to enter into the poorest cottage, though he even creep into it, and though it smell never so lothsomly. For both God is there also, and those for whom God dyed: and so much the rather doth he so, as his accesse to the poor is more comfortable then to the rich; and in regard of himselfe it is more humiliation. These are the parson's general aims in his circuit, but with these he mingles other discourses for conversation sake, and to make his higher purposes slip the more easily.

CHAP. XV

The Parson Comforting

THE countrey parson, when any of his cure is sick, or afflicted with losse of friend or estate, or any ways distressed, fails not to afford his best comforts, and rather goes to them then sends for the afflicted, though they can, and otherwise ought to come to him. To this end he hath thoroughly digested all the points of consolation, as having continuall use of them, such as are from God's generall providence, extended even to lillyes; from His particular to His Church; from His promises; from the examples of all saints that ever were; from Christ Himself, perfecting our redemption no other way then by sorrow; from the benefit of affliction, which softens and works the stubborn heart of man; from the certainty both of deliverance and reward, if we faint not; from the miserable comparison of the moment of griefs here with the weight of joyes hereafter. Besides this, in his visiting the sick or otherwise afflicted he followeth the Churche's counsell, namely, in perswading them to particular confession, labouring to make them understand the great good use of this ancient and pious ordinance, and how necessary it is in some cases; he also urgeth them to do some pious charitable works, as a necessary evidence and fruit of their faith at that time especially; the participation of the holy sacrament, how comfortable and sovereigne a medicine it is to all sin-sick souls, what strength and joy and peace it administers against all temptations, even to death itself, he plainly and generally intimateth to the disaffected or sick person, that so the hunger and thirst after it may come rather from themselves than from his perswasion.

CHAP. XVI

The Parson a Father

THE countrey parson is not only a father to his flock, but also professeth himselfe thoroughly of the opinion, carrying it about with him as fully as if he had begot his whole parish. And of this he makes great use. For by this means, when any sinns, he hateth him not as an officer, but pities him as a father; and even in those wrongs which, either in tithing or otherwise, are done to his owne person, he considers the offender as a child, and forgives, so hee may have any signe of amendment; so also when, after many admonitions, any continue to be refractory, yet hee gives him not over, but is long before hee proceede to disinheriting, or perhaps never goes so far; knowing that some are called at the eleventh houre, and therefore hee still expects and waits, lest he should determine God's houre of coming; which as hee cannot, touching the last day, so neither touching the intermediate days of conversion.

CHAP. XVII

The Parson in Journey

THE countrey parson, when a just occasion calleth him out of his parish (which he diligently and strictly weigheth, his parish being all his joy and thought), leaveth not his ministry behind him; but is himselfe wherever he is. Therefore those he meets on the way he blesseth audibly, and with those he overtakes or that overtake him hee begins good discourses, such as may edify, interposing sometimes some short and honest refreshments, which may make his other discourses more welcome and lesse tedious. And when he comes to his inn, he refuseth not to joyne, that he may enlarge the glory of God to the company he is in, by a due blessing of God for their safe arrival, and saying grace at meat, and at going to bed by giving the host notice that he will have prayers in the hall, wishing him to informe his guests thereof, that if any be willing to partake, they may resort thither. The like he doth in the morning, using pleasantly the outlandish proverb, that 'prayers and provender never hinder journey.' When he comes to any other house, where his kindred or other relations give him any authority over the family, if hee be to stay for a time, hee considers diligently the state thereof to Godward, and that in two points: first, what disorders there are either in apparell, or diet, or too open a buttery, or reading vain books, or swearing, or breeding up children to no calling, but in idleness or the like; secondly, what means of piety, whether daily prayers be used, grace, reading of Scriptures and other good books, how Sundayes, holydays, and fasting-days are kept. And accordingly, as he finds any defect in these, he first considers with himselfe what kind of remedy fits the temper of the house best, and then hee faithfully and boldly applyeth it, yet seasonably and discreetly, by taking aside the lord or lady, or master and mistress of the house, and shewing them cleerly that they respect them most who wish them best, and that not a desire to meddle with others' affairs, but the earnestnesse to do all the good he can, moves him to say thus and thus.

CHAP. XVIII

The Parson in Sentinell

THE countrey parson, wherever he is, keeps God's watch; that is, there is nothing spoken or done in the company where he is, but comes under his test and censure. If it be well spoken or done, he takes occasion to commend and enlarge it; if ill, he presently lays hold of it, lest the poison steal into some young and unwary spirits, and possesse them even before they themselves heed it. But this he doth discreetly, with mollifying and suppling words: 'This was not so well said as it might have been forborn;' 'We cannot allow this:' or else, if the thing will admit interpretation, 'Your meaning is not thus, but thus;' or, 'So far indeed what you say is true, and well said; but this will not stand.' This is called 'keeping God's watch,' when the baits which the enemy lays in company are discovered and avoyded; this is to be on God's side, and be true to His party. Besides, if he perceive in company any discourse tending to ill, either by the wickedness or quarrelsomenesse thereof, he either prevents it judiciously, or breaks it off seasonably by some diversion. Wherein a pleasantness of disposition is of great use, men being willing to sell the interest and engagement of their discourses for no price sooner then that of mirth; whither the nature of man, loving refreshment, gladly betakes itselfe, even to the losse of honour.

CHAP. XIX

The Parson in Reference

THE countrey parson is sincere and upright in all his relations. And first he is just to his countrey; as when he is set at an armour or horse, he borrowes them not to serve the turne, nor provides slight and unusefull, but such as are every way fitting to do his countrey true and laudable service, when occasion requires. To do otherwise is deceit; and therefore not for him, who is hearty, and true in all his wayes, as being the servant of Him 'in Whom there was no guile' [I. Peter ii. 22]. Likewise in any other countrey-duty he considers what is the end of any command, and then he suits things faithfully according to that end. Secondly, he carries himself very respectively as to all the fathers of the Church, so especially to his diocesan, honouring him both in word and behaviour, and resorting unto him in any difficulty, either in his studies or in his parish. He observes visitations, and being there, makes due use of them, as of clergy councils for the benefit of the diocese. And therefore, before he comes having observed some defects in the ministry, he then, either in sermon if he preach, or at some other time of the day, propounds among his brethren what were fitting to be done. Thirdly, he keeps good correspondence with all the neighbouring pastours round about him, performing for them any ministeriall office which is not to the prejudice of his own parish. Likewise he welcomes to his house any minister, how poor or mean soever, with as joyfull a countenance as if he were to entertain some great lord. Fourthly, he fulfills the duty and debt of neighbourhood to all the parishes which are near him; for the Apostle's rule (Philip. iv. [8]) being admirable and large, that we should do 'whatsoever things are honest, or just, or pure, or lovely, or of good report, if there be any virtue or any praise.' And neighbourhood being ever reputed, even among the heathen, as an obligation to do good, rather than to those that are farther, where things are otherwise equall, therefore he satisfies this duty also. Especially if God have sent any calamity, either by fire or famine, to any neighbouring parish, then he expects no brief; but taking his parish together the next Sunday or holyday, and exposing to them the uncertainty of humane affairs, none knowing whose turne may be next, and then when he hath affrighted them with this, exposing the obligation of charity and neighbourhood, he first gives himself liberally, and then incites them to give; making together a summe either to be sent, or, which were more comfortable, all together choosing some fit day to carry it themselves and cheere the afflicted. So, if any neighbouring village be overburdened with poore, and his owne lesse charged, hee finds some way of releeving it, and reducing the manna and bread of charity to some equality; representing to his people that the blessing of God to them ought to make them the more charitable, and not the lesse lest He cast their neighbours' poverty on them also.

CHAP. XX

The Parson in God's Stead

The countrey parson is in God's stead to his parish, and dischargeth God what he can of His promises. Wherefore there is nothing done either wel or ill whereof he is not the rewarder or punisher. If he chance to finde any reading in another's Bible, he provides him one of his own. If he finde another giving a poore man a penny, he gives him a tester for it, if the giver be fit to receive it; or if he be of a condition above such gifts, he sends him a good book, or easeth him in his tithes, telling him when he hath forgotten it, 'This I do, because at such and such a time you were charitable.' This is in some sort a discharging of God as concerning this life, Who hath promised that godliness shall be gainfull; but in the other, God is His own immediate paymaster, rewarding all good deeds to their full proportion. 'The parson's punishing of sin and vice is rather by withdrawing his bounty and courtesie from the parties offending, or by private or publick reproof, as the case requires, then by causing them to be presented or otherwise complained of. And yet, as the malice of the person or heinousness of the crime may be, he is carefull to see condign punishment inflicted, and with truly godly zeal, without hatred to the person, hungereth and thirsteth after righteous punishment of unrighteousnesse. Thus both in rewarding vertue and in punishing vice, the parson endeavoureth to be in God's stead, knowing that countrey people are drawn or led by sense more then by faith, by present rewards or punishments more then by future.'

CHAP. XXI

The Parson Catechizing

THE countrey parson values catechizing highly; for there being three points of his duty—the one, to infuse a competent knowledge of salvation in every one of his flock; the other to multiply and build up this knowledge to a spirituall temple; the third, to inflame this knowledge, to presse and drive it to practice, turning it to reformation of life by pithy and lively exhortations—catechizing is the first point, and but by catechizing the other cannot be attained. Besides, whereas in sermons there is a kinde of state, in catechizing there is an humblenesse very suitable to Christian regeneration; which exceedingly delights him as by way of exercise upon himself, and by way of preaching to himselfe, for the advancing of his own mortification; for in preaching to others he forgets not himself, but is first a sermon to himself, and then to others, growing with the growth of his parish. He useth and preferreth the ordinary Church Catechism, partly for obedience to authority, partly for uniformity sake, that the same common truths may be everywhere professed, especially since many remove from parish to parish, who, like Christian souldiers, are to give the word and to satisfy the congregation by their Catholic answers. He exacts of all the doctrine of the Catechisme: of the younger sort, the very words; of the elder, the substance. Those he catechizeth publickly, these privately, giving age honour, according to the Apostle's rule (I. Tim. v. 1). He requires all to be present at catechizing: first, for the authority of the work; secondly, that parents and masters, as they hear the answers prove, may, when they come home, either commend or reprove, either reward or punish; thirdly, that those of the elder sort, who are not well grounded, may then by an honourable way take occasion to be better instructed; fourthly, that those who are well grown in the knowledge of religion may examine their grounds, renew their vowes, and by occasion of both inlarge their meditations. When once all have learned the words of the Catechisme, he thinks it the most usefull way that a parson can take to go over the same, but in other words; for many say the Catechisme by rote, as parrats, without ever piercing into the sense of it. In this course the order of the Catechism would be kept, but the rest varyed: as thus in the Creed: 'How came this world to be as it is? Was it made, or came it by chance? Who made it? Did you see God make it? Then are there some things to be beleeved that are not seen? Is this the nature of beliefe? Is not Christianity full of such things, as are not to be seen, but beleeved? You said God made the world; who is God?' And so forward, requiring answers to all these, and helping and cherishing the answerer, by making the questions very plaine with comparisons, and making much even of a word of truth from him. This order being used to one, would be a little varyed to another. And this is an admirable way of teaching, wherein the catechized will at length find delight, and by which the catechizer, if he once get the skill of it, will draw out of ignorant and silly souls even the dark and deep points of religion. Socrates did thus in philosophy, who held that the seeds of all truths lay in every body, and accordingly, by questions well ordered, he found philosophy in silly tradesmen. That position will not hold in Christianity, because it contains things above nature; but after that the Catechisme is once learn'd, that which nature is towards philosophy the Catechism is towards divinity. To this purpose, some dialogues in Plato were worth the reading, where the singular dexterity of Socrates in this kind may be observed and imitated. Yet the skill consists but in these three points: First, an aim and mark of the whole discourse whither to drive the answerer, which the questionist must have in his mind before any question be propounded, upon which and to which the questions are to be chained. Secondly, a most plain and easie framing the question, even containing in vertue the answer also, especially to the more ignorant. Thirdly, when the answerer sticks, in illustrating the thing by something else which he knows, making what he knows to serve him in that which he knows not: as when the parson once demanded, after other questions about man's misery, 'Since man is so miserable, what is to be done?' and the answerer could not tell, he asked him again what he would do if he were in a ditch. This familiar illustration made the answer so plaine, that he was even ashamed of his ignorance; for he could not but say he would haste out of it as fast as he could. Then he proceeded to ask whether he could get out of the ditch alone, or whether he needed a helper, and who was that helper. This is the skill, and doubtlesse the Holy Scripture intends thus much when it condescends to the naming of a plough, a hatchet, a bushell, leaven, boyes piping and dancing; shewing that things of ordinary use are not only to serve in the way of drudgery, but to be washed and cleansed, and serve for lights even of heavenly truths. This is the practice which the parson so much commends to all his fellow-labourers; the secret of whose good consists in this—that at sermons and prayers men may sleep or wander; but when one is asked a question, he must discover what he is. This practice exceeds even sermons in teaching: but there being two things in sermons, the one informing, the other inflaming; as sermons come short of questions in the one, so they far exceed them in the other. For questions cannot inflame or ravish; that must be done by a set, and laboured, and continued speech.

CHAP. XXII

The Parson in Sacraments

The countrey parson being to administer the sacraments is at a stand with himself how or what behaviour to assume for so holy things. Especially at communion times he is in a great confusion, as being not only to receive God, but to break and administer Him. Neither finds he any issue in this, but to throw himself down at the throne of grace, saying, ‘Lord, Thou knowest what Thou didst when Thou appointedst it to be done thus; therefore doe Thou fulfill what Thou dost appoint; for Thou art not only the feast, but the way to it.’ At Baptisme, being himselfe in white, he requires the presence of all, and baptizeth not willingly, but on Sundayes or great dayes. Hee admits no vaine or idle names, but such as are usuall and accustomed. Hee says that prayer with great devotion where God is thanked for ‘calling us to the knowledg of His grace,’ Baptisme being a blessing that the world hath not the like. He willingly and cheerfully crosseth the child, and thinketh the ceremony not only innocent, but reverend. He instructeth the godfathers and godmothers that it is no complementall or light thing to sustain that place, but a great honour, and no less burden, as being done both in the presence of God and His Saints, and by way of undertaking for a Christian soul. He adviseth all to call to mind their baptism often; for if wise men have thought it the best way of preserving a State to reduce it to its principles by which it grew great, certainly it is the safest course for Christians also to meditate on their baptisme often (being the first step into their great and glorious calling), and upon what termes and with what vows they were baptized. At the times of the Holy Communion he first takes order with the church-wardens, that the elements be of the best, not cheape or course, much less ill-tasted or unwholsome. Secondly, he considers and looks into the ignorance or carelessness of his flock, and accordingly applies himself with catechizings and lively exhortations, not on the Sunday of the communion only (for then it is too late), but the Sunday or Sundayes before the communion, or on the eves of all those dayes. If there be any, who having not received yet, is to enter into this great work, he takes the more pains with them, that hee may lay the foundation of future blessings. The time of every one's first receiving is not so much by yeers as by understanding: particularly the rule may be this: when any one can distinguish the sacramentall from common bread, knowing the institution and the difference, hee ought to receive, of what age soever. Children and youths are usually deferred too long, under pretence of devotion to the sacrament; but it is for want of instruction; their understandings being ripe enough for ill things, and why not then for better? But parents and masters should make hast in this, as to a great purchase for their children and servants; which, while they deferr, both sides suffer—the one, in wanting many excitings of grace; the other, in being worse served and obeyed. The saying of the Catechism is necessary, but not enough, because to answer in form may still admit ignorance; but the questions must be propounded loosely and wildely, and then the answerer will discover what hee is. Thirdly, for the manner of receiving, as the parson useth all reverence himself, so he administers to none but to the reverent. The feast indeed requires sitting, because it is a feast; but man's unpreparednesse asks kneeling. Hee that comes to the sacrament hath the confidence of a guest, and hee that kneels confesseth himself an unworthy one, and therefore differs from other feasters: but hee that sits or lies puts up to an Apostle; contentiousnesse in a feast of charity is more scandall than any posture. Fourthly, touching the frequency of the Communion, the parson celebrates it, if not duly once a month, yet at least five or six times in the year: as at Easter, Christmasse, Whitsuntide, afore and after harvest, and the beginning of Lent. And this hee doth not onely for the benefit of the work, but also for the discharge of the church-wardens, who, being to present all that receive not thrice a year, if there be but three communions, neither can all the people so order their affairs as to receive just at those times, nor the churchwardens so well take notice who receive thrice, and who not.

CHAP. XXIII

The Parson's Completenesse

THE countrey parson desires to be all to his parish, and not only a pastour, but a lawyer also and a phisitian. Therefore hee endures not that any of his flock should go to law; but in any controversie that they should resort to him as their judg. To this end he hath gotten to himself some insight in things ordinarily incident and controverted, by experience and by reading some initiatory treatises in the law, with Dalton's 'Justice of Peace' and the 'Abridgements of the Statutes,' as also by discourse with men of that profession whom he hath ever some cases to ask when he meets with them; holding that rule, that to put men to discourse of that wherein they are most eminent is the most gainfull way of conversation. Yet whenever any controversie is brought to him, he never decides it alone; but sends for three or four of the ablest of the parish to hear the cause with him, whom he makes to deliver their opinion first; out of which he gathers, in case he be ignorant himself, what to hold; and so the thing passeth with more authority and lesse envy. In judging, he followes that which is altogether right; so that if the poorest man of the parish detain but a pin unjustly from the richest, he absolutely restores it as a judge; but when he hath so done, then he assumes the parson and exhorts to charity. Nevertheless, there may happen sometimes some cases wherein he chooseth to permit his parishioners rather to make use of the law than himself: as in cases of an obscure and dark nature, not easily determinable by lawyers themselves; or in cases of high consequence, as establishing of inheritances; or lastly, when the persons in difference are of a contentious disposition, and cannot be gained, but that they still fall from all compromises that have been made. But then he shows them how to go to law even as brethren, and not as enemies; neither avoyding therefore one another's company, much lesse defaming one another. Now as the parson is in law, so is he in sicknesse also; if there be any of his flock sick, hee is their physician, or at least his wife, of whom, instead of the qualities of the world, he asks no other but to have the skill of healing a wound or helping the sick. But if neither himselfe nor his wife have the skil, and his means serve, he keepes some young practitioner in his house for the benefit of his parish, whom yet he ever exhorts not to exceed his bounds, but in tickle cases to call in help. If all fail, then he keeps good correspondence with some neighbour phisician, and entertaines him for the cure of his parish. Yet it is easie for any scholar to attaine to such a measure of physick as may be of much use to him both for himself and others. This is done by seeing one anatomy, reading one book of physick, having one herball by him. And let Fernelius be the physick author, for he writes briefly, neatly, and judiciously; especially let his method of physick be diligently perused, as being the practicall part, and of most use. Now both the reading of him and the knowing of herbs may be done at such times as they may be an help and a recreation to more divine studies, Nature serving grace both in comfort of diversion and the benefit of application when need requires, as also by way of illustration, even as our Saviour made plants and seeds to teach the people; for He was the true householder who bringeth out of His treasure things new and old—the old things of philosophy and the new of grace—and maketh the one serve the other. And I conceive our Saviour did this for three reasons: first, that by familiar things Hee might make His doctrine slip the more easily into the hearts even of the meanest; secondly, that labouring people (whom He chiefly considered) might have everywhere monuments of His doctrine, remembring in gardens His mustard-seed and lillyes, in the field His seed-corn and tares, and so not be drowned altogether in the works of their vocation, but sometimes lift up their minds to better things, even in the midst of their pains; thirdly, that He might set a copy for parsons. In the knowledge of simples, wherein the manifold wisdom of God is wonderfully to be seen, one thing would be carefully observed; which is, to know what herbs may be used instead of drugs of the same nature, and to make the garden the shop. For home-bred medicines are both more easie for the parson's purse, and more familiar for all men's bodyes. So where the apothecary useth either for loosing, rhubarb, or for binding, bolearmena, the parson useth damask or white roses for the one, and plantaine, shepherd's purse, knot-grasse for the other, and that with better successe. As for spices, he doth not only prefer home-bred things before them, but condemns them for vanities, and so shuts them out of his family, esteeming that there is no spice comparable for herbs to rosemary, thyme, savory, mints; and for seeds, to fennell and carroway-seeds. Accordingly for salves his wife seeks not the city, but prefers her garden and fields before all outlandish gums. And surely hyssope, valerian, mercury, adder's tongue, yerrow, melilot, and St. John's wort made into a salve, and elder, camomill, mallowes, comphrey, and smallage made into a poultis, have done great and rare cures. In curing of any, the parson and his family use to premise prayers; for this is to cure like a parson, and this raiseth the action from the shop to the church. But though the parson sets forward all charitable deeds, yet he looks not in this point of curing beyond his own parish, except the person be so poor that he is not able to reward the physician; for as hee is charitable, so he is just also. Now it is a justice and debt to the commonwealth he lives in not to incroach on others' professions, but to live on his own. And justice is the ground of charity.

CHAP. XXIV

The Parson's Arguing

The countrey parson, if there be any of his parish that hold strange doctrins, useth all possible diligence to reduce them to the common faith. The first means he useth is prayer, beseeching the Father of lights to open their eyes, and to give him power so to fit his discourse to them that it may effectually pierce their hearts and convert them. The second means is a very loving and sweet usage of them, both in going to and sending for them often, and in finding out courtesies to place on them, as in their tithes or otherwise. The third means is the observation what is the main foundation and pillar of their cause wherein they rely; as if he be a papist, the Church is the hinge he turns on; if a schismatick, scandall. Wherefore the parson hath diligently examined these two with himselfe: as what the Church is, how it began, how it proceeded; whether it be a rule to itselfe; whether it hath a rule; whether having a rule it ought not to be guided by it; whether any rule in the world be obscure; and how then should the best be so, at least in fundamental things, the obscurity in some points being the exercise of the Church, the light in the foundations being the guide; the Church needing both an evidence and an exercise. So for scandall: what scandall is, when given or taken; whether, there being two precepts, one of obeying authority, the other of not giving scandall, that ought not to be preferred, especially since in disobeying there is scandall also; whether things once indifferent being made by the precept of authority more then indifferent, it be in our power to omit or refuse them. These and the like points hee hath accurately digested, having ever besides two great helps and powerful perswaders on his side: the one a strict religious life; the other an humble and ingenuous search of truth; being unmoved in arguing, and voyd of all contentiousnesse, which are two great lights able to dazzle the eyes of the misled, while they consider that God cannot be wanting to them in doctrine to whom He is so gracious in life.

CHAP. XXV

The Parson Punishing

WHENSOEVER the countrey parson proceeds so farre as to call in authority, and to do such things of legall opposition either in the presenting or punishing of any as the vulgar every consters for signes of ill will, he forbears not in any wise to use the delinquent as before in his behaviour and carriage towards him, not avoyding his company, or doing anything of aversenesse, save in the very act of punishment; neither doth he esteem him for an enemy, but as a brother still, except some small and temporary estranging may corroborate the punishment to a better subduing and humbling of the delinquent; which if it happily take effect, he then comes on the faster, and makes so much the more of him as before he alienated himselfe, doubling his regards, and shewing by all means that the delinquent's return is to his advantage.

CHAP. XXVI

The Parson's Eye

THE countrey parson at spare times from action, standing on a hill, and considering his flock, discovers two sorts of vices and two sorts of vicious persons. There are some vices whose natures are alwayes clear and evident, as adultery, murder, hatred, lying, &c. There are other vices whose natures, at least in the beginning, are dark and obscure, as covetousnesse and gluttony. So likewise there are some persons who abstain not even from known sins. There are others who, when they know a sin evidently, they commit it not. It is true, indeed, they are long a-knowing it, being partiall to themselves, and witty to others who shall reprove them from it. A man may be both covetous and intemperate, and yet hear sermons against both, and himselfe condemn both in good earnest; and the reason hereof is, because the natures of these vices being not evidently discussed, or known commonly, the beginnings of them are not easily observable; and the beginnings of them are not observed, because of the suddain passing from that which was just now lawfull to that which is presently unlawfull, even in one continued action. So a man dining, eats at first lawfully; but proceeding on, comes to do unlawfully, even before he is aware, not knowing the bounds of the action, nor when his eating begins to be unlawfull. So a man storing up mony for his necessary provisions, both in present for his family and in future for his children, hardly perceives when his storing becomes unlawfull; yet is there a period for his storing, and a point or center when his storing, which was even now good, passeth from good to bad. Wherefore the parson, being true to his businesse, hath exactly sifted the definitions of all vertues and vices; especially canvassing those whose natures are most stealing and beginnings uncertain. Particularly concerning these two vices, not because they are all that are of this dark and creeping disposition, but for example sake, and because they are most common, he thus thinks: first, for covetousnes, he lays this ground—whosoever, when a just occasion cals, either spends not at all, or not in some proportion to God's blessing upon him, is covetous. The reason of the ground is manifest, because wealth is given to that end, to supply our occasions. Now, if I do not give everything its end, I abuse the creature, I am false to my reason which should guide me, I offend the supreme Judg, in perverting that order which He hath set both to things and to reason. The application of the ground would be infinite; but in brief, a poor man is an occasion, my countrey is an occasion, my friend is an occasion, my table is an occasion, my apparell is an occasion: if in all these, and those more which concerne me, I either do nothing, or pinch and scrape and squeeze blood indecently to the station wherein God hath placed me, I am covetous. More particularly, and to give one instance for all, if God have given me servants, and I either provide too little for them, or that which is unwholsome, being sometimes baned meat, sometimes too salt, and so not competent nourishment, I am covetous. I bring this example, because men usually think that servants for their mony are as other things that they buy, even as a piece of wood, which they may cut, or hack, or throw into the fire; and so they pay them their wages, all is well. Nay, to descend yet more particularly, if a man hath wherewithall to buy a spade, and yet hee chuseth rather to use his neighbour's, and wear out that, he is covetous. Nevertheless, few bring covetousness thus low, or consider it so narrowly; which yet ought to be done, since there is a justice in the least things, and for the least there shall be a judgment. Countrey people are full of these petty injustices, being cunning to make use of another, and spare themselves; and scholers ought to be diligent in the observation of these, and driving of their generall school-rules ever to the smallest actions of life; which while they dwell in their bookes they will never finde, but being seated in the countrey, and doing their duty faithfully, they will soon discover; especially if they carry their eyes ever open, and fix them on their charge, and not on their preferment. Secondly, for gluttony, the parson lays this ground—he that either for quantity eats more than his health or imployments will bear, or for quality is licorous after dainties, is a glutton; as he that eats more than his estate will bear is a prodigall; and hee that eats offensively to the company, either in his order or length of eating, is scandalous and uncharitable. These three rules generally comprehend the faults of eating, and the truth of them needs no proof; so that men must eat neither to the disturbance of their health, nor of their affairs (which being over-burdened, or studying dainties too much, they cannot wel dispatch), nor of their estate, nor of their brethren. One act in these things is bad, but it is the custom and habit that names a glutton. Many think they are at more liberty then they are, as if they were masters of their health, and so they will stand to the pain, all is well. But to eat to one's hurt comprehends, besides the hurt, an act against reason, because it is unnaturall to hurt oneself; and this they are not masters of. Yet of hurtfull things, I am more bound to abstain from those which by my own experience I have found hurtfull, then from those which by a common tradition and vulgar knowledge are reputed to be so. That which is said of hurtfull meats extends to hurtfull drinks also. As for the quantity, touching our imployments, none must eat so as to disable themselves from a fit discharging either of divine duties or duties of their calling. So that if after dinner they are not fit (or unweeldy) either to pray or work, they are gluttons. Not that all must presently work after dinner (for they rather must not work, especially students and those that are weakly); but that they must rise so as that it is not meate or drink that hinders them from working. To guide them in this there are three rules: first, the custome and knowledge of their own body, and what it can well digest; the second, the feeling of themselves in time of eating, which because it is deceitfull (for one thinks in eating that he can eat more then afterwards he finds true); the third is the observation with what appetite they sit down. This last rule joyned with the first never fails; for knowing what one usually can digest, and feeling when I go to meat in what disposition I am, either hungry or not, according as I feele myself, either I take my wonted proportion, or diminish of it. Yet phisicians bid those that would live in health not keep an uniform diet, but to feed variously, now more, now lesse; and Gerson, a spirituall man, wisheth all to incline rather to too much then to too little; his reason is, because diseases of exinanition are more dangerous than diseases of repletion. But the parson distinguisheth according to his double aime, either of abstinence a morall vertue, or mortification a divine. When he deals with any that is heavy and carnall, he gives him those freer rules; but when he meets with a refined and heavenly disposition, he carryes them higher, even somtimes to a forgetting of themselves, knowing there is One Who, when they forget, remembers for them; as when the people hungered and thirsted after our Saviour's doctrine, and tarryed so long at it, that they would have fainted had they returned empty, He suffered it not; but rather made food miraculously, then suffered so good desires to miscarry.

CHAP. XXVII

The Parson in Mirth

The countrey parson is generally sad, because hee knows nothing but the Crosse of Christ, his minde being defixed on and with those nailes wherewith his Master was; or if he have any leisure to look off from thence, he meets continually with two most sad spectacles, sin and misery; God dishonoured every day, and man afflicted. Neverthelesse, he somtimes refresheth himself, as knowing that nature will not bear everlasting droopings, and that pleasantnesse of disposition is a great key to do good; not onely because all men shun the company of perpetuall severity, but also for that when they are in company, instructions seasoned with pleasantnesse both enter sooner and roote deeper. Wherefore he condescends to humane frailities both in himselfe and others, and intermingles some mirth in his discourses occasionally, according to the pulse of the hearer.

CHAP. XXVIII

The Parson in Contempt

THE countrey parson knows well, that both for the generall ignominy which is cast upon the profession, and much more for those rules which out of his choycest judgment hee hath resolved to observe, and which are described in this book, he must be depised, because this hath been the portion of God his Master and of God's saints his brethren; and this is foretold that it shall be so still, until things be no more. Neverthelesse, according to the Apostle's rule, he endeavours that 'none shall despise him' [Titus ii. 15]; especially in his own parish he suffers it not to his utmost power, for that where contempt is there is no room for instruction. This he procures—first, by his holy and unblameable life, which carries a reverence with it even above contempt. Secondly, by a courteous carriage and winning behaviour; he that wil be respected must respect, doing kindnesses, but receiving none, at least of those who are apt to despise; for this argues a height and eminency of mind which is not easily despised, except it degenerate to pride. Thirdly, by a bold and impartial reproof even of the best in the parish, when occasion requires; for this may produce hatred in those that are reproved, but never contempt either in them or others. Lastly, if the contempt shall proceed so far as to do anything punishable by law, as contempt is apt to do if it be not thwarted, 'the parson having a due respect both to the person and to the cause, referreth the whole matter to the examination and punishment of those which are in authority,' that so the sentence lighting upon one the example may reach to all. But if the contempt be not punishable by law, or being so, the parson think it in his discretion either unfit or bootlesse to contend, then when any despises him, he takes it either in an humble way, saying nothing at all; or else in a slighting way, shewing that reproaches touch him no more then a stone thrown against heaven, where he is and lives; or in a sad way, grieved at his own and others' sins, which continually breake God's laws, and dishonour Him with those mouths which he continually fills and feeds; or else in a doctrinal way, saying to the contemner, 'Alas, why do you thus? You hurt yourselfe, not me; he that throws a stone at another hits himselfe;' and so between gentle reasoning and pitying he overcomes the evil; or lastly, in a triumphant way, being glad and joyfull, that he is made conformable to his Master, and being in the world as He was, hath this undoubted pledge of his salvation. These are the five shields wherewith the godly receive the darts of the wicked, leaving anger and retorting and revenge to the children of the world, whom another's ill mastereth and leadeth captive without any resistance, even in resistance, to the same destruction. For while they resist the person that reviles, they resist not the evill which takes hold of them, and is farr the worst enemy.

CHAP. XXIX

The Parson with his Church-Wardens

The countrey parson doth often, both publickly and privately, instruct his church-wardens what a great charge lyes upon them, and that, indeed, the whole order and discipline of the parish is put into their hands. If himselfe reform anything, it is out of the overflowing of his conscience; whereas they are to do it by command and by oath. Neither hath the place its dignity from the ecclesiastical laws only, since even by the common statute-law they are taken for a kinde of corporation, as being persons enabled by that name to take moveable goods or chattels, and to sue and be sued at law concerning such goods for the use and profit of their parish; and by the same law they are to levy penalties for negligence in resorting to church, or for disorderly carriage in time of divine service. Wherefore the parson suffers not the place to be vilified or debased by being cast on the lower ranke of people; but invites and urges the best unto it, shewing that they do not loose or go lesse, but gaine by it, it being the greatest honour of this world to do God and His chosen service, or, as David says, to be even a doorkeeper in the house of God. Now the canons being the church-warden's rule, the parson adviseth them to read or hear them read often, as also the visitation articles, which are grounded upon the canons, that so they may know their duty and keep their oath the better; in which regard, considering the great consequence of their place, and more of their oath, he wisheth them by no means to spare any, though never so great; but if after gentle and neighbourly admonitions they still persist in ill, to present them, yea, though they be tenants, or otherwise ingaged to the delinquent; for their obligation to God and their own soul is above any temporal tye. Do well and right, and let the world sink.

CHAP. XXX

The Parson's Consideration of Providence

The countrey parson, considering the great aptnesse countrey people have to think that all things come by a kind of natural course, and that if they sow and soyle their grounds they must have corn, if they keep and fodder well their cattel they must have milk and calves; labours to reduce them to see God's hand in all things, and to beleeve that things are not set in such an inevitable order, but that God often changeth it according as He sees fit, either for reward or punishment. To this end he represents to his flock that God hath and exerciseth a threefold power in everything which concernes man. The first is a sustaining power, the second a governing power, the third a spirituall power. By His sustaining power He preserves and actuates every thing in his being, so that corne doth not grow by any other vertue then by that which He continually supplyes as the corne needs it; without which supply the corne would instantly dry up, as a river would if the fountain were stopped. And it is observable that if any thing could presume of an inevitable course and constancy in their operations, certainly it should be either the sun in heaven or the fire on earth, by reason of their fierce, strong, and violent natures; yet when God pleased the sun stood still, the fire burned not. By God's governing power He preserves and orders the references of things one to the other, so that though the corn do grow and be preserved in that act by His sustaining power, yet if he suite not other things to the growth, as seasons and weather, and other accidents, by His governing power, the fairest harvests come to nothing. And it is observable that God delights to have men feel and acknowledge and reverence His power, and therefore He often overturnes things when they are thought past danger; that is His time of interposing: as when a merchant hath a ship come home after many a storme, which it hath escaped, He destroyes it sometimes in the very haven; or if the goods be housed, a fire hath broken forth and suddenly consumed them. Now this He doth that men should perpetuate and not break off their acts of dependence, how fair soever the opportunities present themselves. So that if a farmer should depend upon God all the yeer, and being ready to put hand to sickle shall then secure himself, and think all cock-sure, then God sends such weather as lays the corn and destroys it; or if he depend on God further, even till he imbarn his corn, and then think all sure, God sends a fire and consumes all that he hath; for that he ought not to break off, but to continue his dependance on God, not onely before the corn is inned, but after also, and indeed to depend and fear continually. The third power is spirituall, by which God turnes all outward blessings to inward advantages. So that if a farmer hath both a faire harvest, and that also well inned and imbarned and continuing safe there, yet if God give him not the grace to use and utter this well, all his advantages are to his losse. Better were his corne burnt then not spiritually improved. And it is observable in this how God's goodnesse strives with man's refractorinesse: man would sit down at this world; God bids him sell it and purchase a better. Just as a father who hath in his hand an apple and a piece of gold under it; the child comes, and with pulling gets the apple out of his father's hand; his father bids him throw it away, and he will give him the gold for it; which the child utterly refusing, eats it, and is troubled with wormes. So is the carnall and wilfull man, with the worm of the grave in this world and the worm of conscience in the next.

CHAP. XXXI

The Parson in Liberty

The countrey parson observing the manifold wiles of Satan, who playes his part sometimes in drawing God's servants from Him, sometimes in perplexing them in the service of God, stands fast in 'the liberty wherewith Christ hath made us free' [Galatians v. 1]. This liberty he compasseth by one distinction, and that is of what is necessary and what is additionary. As for example: it is necessary that all Christians should pray twice a day every day of the week, and four times on Sunday, if they be well. This is so necessary and essentiall to a Christian that he cannot without this maintain himself in a Christian state. Besides this, the godly have ever added some houres of prayer, as at nine, or at three, or at midnight, or as they think fit and see cause, or rather as God's Spirit leads them. But these prayers are not necessary, but additionary. Now it so happens that the godly petitioner upon some emergent interruption in the day or by oversleeping himself at night, omits his additionary prayer. Upon this his mind begins to be perplexed and troubled; and Satan, who knows the exigent, blows the fire, endeavouring to disorder the Christian and put him out of his station, and to enlarge the perplexity until it spread, and taint his other duties of piety, which none can perform so well in trouble as in calmness. Here the parson interposeth with his distinction, and shews the perplexed Christian that this prayer being additionary, not necessary, taken in, not commanded, the omission thereof upon just occasion ought by no means to trouble him. God knows the occasion as well as he, and He is as a gracious Father, who more accepts a common course of devotion than dislikes an occasional interruption. And of this he is so to assure himself as to admit no scruple, but to go on as cheerfully as if he had not been interrupted. By this it is evident that the distinction is of singular use and comfort, especially to pious minds, which are ever tender and delicate. But here there are two cautions to be added: first, that this interruption proceed not out of slacknes or coldness, which will appear if the pious soul foresee and prevent such interruptions, what he may, before they come, and when for all that they do come he be a little affected therewith, but not afflicted or troubled, if he resent it to a mislike, but not a griefe; secondly, that this interruption proceede not out of shame. As for example: a godly man, not out of superstition, but of reverence to God's house, resolves, whenever he enters into a church, to kneel down and pray, either blessing God that He will be pleased to dwell among men, or beseeching Him that whenever he repairs to His house he may behave himself so as befits so great a presence, and this briefly. But it happens that neer the place where he is to pray he spyes some scoffing ruffian, who is likely to deride him for his paines; if he now shall either for fear or shame break his custome, he shall do passing ill; so much the rather ought he to proceed, as that by this he may take into his prayer humiliation also. On the other side, if I am to visit the sick in haste, and my neerest way lie through the church, I will not doubt to go without staying to pray there—but onely, as I pass, in my heart—because this kinde of prayer is additionary, not necessary, and the other duty overweighs it; so that if any scruple arise, I will throw it away, and be most confident that God is not displeased. This distinction may run through all Christian duties, and it is a great stay and setling to religious souls.

CHAP. XXXII

The Parson's Surveys

The countrey parson hath not onely taken a particular survey of the faults of his own parish, but a generall also of the diseases of the time, that so, when his occasions carry him abroad or bring strangers to him, he may be the better armed to encounter them. The great and national sin of this Land he esteems to be idlenesse, great in itselfe and great in consequence; for when men have nothing to do, then they fall to drink, to steal, to whore, to scoffe, to revile, to all sorts of gamings. 'Come,' say they, 'we have nothing to do; let's go to the tavern, or to the stews, or what not.' Wherefore the parson strongly opposeth this sin wheresoever he goes. And because idleness is twofold, the one in having no calling, the other in walking carelessly in our calling, he first represents to every body the necessity of a vocation. The reason of this assertion is taken from the nature of man, wherein God hath placed two great instruments, reason in the soul and a hand in the body, as ingagements of working, so that even in Paradise man had a calling; and how much more out of Paradise, when the evills which he is now subject unto may be prevented or diverted by reasonable imployment! Besides, every gift or ability is a talent to be accounted for, and to be improved to our Master's advantage. Yet it is also a debt to our countrey to have a calling, and it concernes the commonwealth that none shall be idle, but all busied. Lastly, riches are the blessing of God, and the great instrument of doing admirable good; therefore all are to procure them honestly and seasonably when they are not better imployed. Now this reason crosseth not our Saviour's precept of selling what we have, because when we have sold all and given it to the poor we must not be idle, but labour to get more, that we may give more, according to St. Paul's rule (Ephesians iv. 28; I. Thessalonians iv. 11, 12); so that our Saviour's selling is so far from crossing St. Paul's working that it rather establisheth it, since they that have nothing are fittest to work. Now because the onely opposer to this doctrine is the gallant, who is witty enough to abuse both others and himself, and who is ready to ask if he shall mend shoes, or what he shall do, therefore the parson unmoved sheweth that ingenuous and fit employment is never wanting to those that seek it. But if it should be, the assertion stands thus: all are either to have a calling or prepare for it; he that hath or can have yet no imployment, if he truly and seriously prepare for it, he is safe and within bounds. Wherefore all are either presently to enter into a calling, if they be fit for it and it for them, or else to examine with care and advice what they are fittest for, and to prepare for that with all diligence. But it will not be amisse in this exceeding useful point to descend to particulars; for exactnesse lyes in particulars. Men are either single or marryed; the marryed and housekeeper hath his hands full, if he do what he ought to do. For there are two branches of his affaires: first, the improvement of his family, by bringing them up in the fear and nurture of the Lord; and secondly, the improvement of his grounds, by drowning, or draining, or stocking, or fencing, and ordering his land to the best advantage both of himself and his neighbours. The Italian says, 'None fouls his hands in his own business;' and it is an honest and just care, so it exceed not bounds, for every one to imploy himself to the advancement of his affairs, that he may have wherewithall to do good. But his family is his best care, to labour Christian soules, and raise them to their height, even to heaven; to dresse and prune them, and take as much joy in a straight-growing childe or servant as a gardiner doth in a choice tree. Could men finde out this delight, they would seldome be from home; whereas now, of any place they are least there. But if, after all this care well dispatched, the housekeeper's family be so small and his dexterity so great that he have leisure to look out, the village or parish which either he lives in or is near unto it is his imployment. Hee considers every one there, and either helps them in particular, or hath generall propositions to the whole towne or hamlet of advancing the publick stock, and managing commons or woods, according as the place suggests. But if hee may be of the commission of peace, there is nothing to that; no commonwealth in the world hath a braver institution than that of justices of the peace; for it is both a security to the king, who hath so many dispersed officers at his beck throughout the kingdome accountable for the publick good, and also an honourable imployment of a gentle or nobleman in the country he lives in, inabling him with power to do good, and to restrain all those who else might both trouble him and the whole State. Wherefore it behoves all who are come to the gravitie and ripenesse of judgment for so excellent a place not to refuse, but rather to procure it. And whereas there are usually three objections made against the place—the one, the abuse of it, by taking petty countrey-bribes; the other, the casting of it on mean persons, especially in some shires; and lastly, the trouble of it—these are so far from deterring any good man from the place, that they kindle them rather to redeem the dignity either from true faults or unjust aspersions. Now for single men, they are either heirs or younger brothers: the heirs are to prepare in all the fore-mentioned points against the time of their practice. Therefore they are to mark their father's discretion in ordering his house and affairs, and also elsewhere when they see any remarkable point of education or good husbandry, and to transplant it in time to his own home, with the same care as others, when they meet with good fruit, get a graffe of the tree, inriching their orchard and neglecting their house. Besides, they are to read books of law and justice, especially the statutes at large. As for better books of divinity, they are not in this consideration, because we are about a calling and a preparation thereunto. But chiefly, and above all things, they are to frequent sessions and assizes; for it is both an honor which they owe to the reverend judges and magistrates to attend them at least in their shire, and it is a great advantage to know the practice of the Land, for our law is practice. Sometimes he may go to court, as the eminent place both of good and ill. At other times he is to travell over the king's dominions, cutting out the kingdome into portions, which every yeer he surveys peecemeal. When there is a Parliament, he is to endeavour by all means to be a knight or burgess there; for there is no school to a Parliament. And when he is there, he must not only be a morning man, but at committees also; for there the particulars are exactly discussed, which are brought from thence to the House but in generall. When none of these occasions call him abroad, every morning that hee is at home hee must either ride the great horse or exercise some of his military gestures. For all gentlemen that are not weakned and disarmed with sedentary lives are to know the use of their arms; and as the husbandman labours for them, so must they fight for and defend them when occasion calls. This is the duty of each to other, which they ought to fulfill; and the parson is a lover and exciter to justice in all things, even as John the Baptist squared out to every one, even to soldiers, what to do. As for younger brothers, those whom the parson finds loose and not engaged in some profession by their parents, whose neglect in this point is intolerable and a shamefull wrong both to the commonwealth and their own house—to them, after he hath shewd the unlawfulness of spending the day in dressing, complementing, visiting, and sporting, he first commends the study of the Civill Law, as a brave and wise knowledg, the professours whereof were much imployed by Queen Elizabeth, because it is the key of commerce, and discovers the rules of forraine nations. Secondly, he commends the mathematicks, as the only wonder-working knowledg, and therefore requiring the best spirits. After the severall knowledge of these, he adviseth to insist and dwell chiefly on the two noble branches thereof of fortification and navigation; the one being usefull to all countreys, and the other especially to ilands. But if the young gallant think these courses dull and phlegmatick, where can he busie himself better then in those new Plantations and discoveryes, which are not only a noble, but also, as they may be handled, a religious imployment? Or let him travel into Germany and France, and observing the artifices and manufactures there, transplant them hither, as divers have done lately, to our countrey's advantage.

CHAP. XXXIII

The Parson's Library

The countrey parson's library is a holy life; for besides the blessing that that brings upon it, there being a promise that if the kingdome of God be first sought, 'all other things shall be added' [St. Matthew vi. 32], even itselfe is a sermon. For the temptations with which a good man is beset, and the ways which he used to overcome them, being told to another, whether in private conference or in the church, are a sermon. Hee that hath considered how to carry himself at table about his appetite, if he tell this to another, preacheth; and much more feelingly and judiciously then he writes his rules of temperance out of bookes; so that the parson having studied and mastered all his lusts and affections within, and the whole army of temptations without, hath ever so many sermons ready penn'd as he hath victories. And it fares in this as it doth in physick; he that hath been sick of a consumption, and knows what recovered him, is a physitian, so far as he meetes with the same disease and temper, and can much better and particularly do it then he that is generally learned and was never sick. And if the same person had been sick of all diseases, and were recovered of all by things that he knew, there were no such physician as he, both for skill and tendernesse. Just so it is in divinity, and that not without manifest reason; for though the temptations may be diverse in divers Christians, yet the victory is alike in all, being by the self-same Spirit. Neither is this true onely in the military state of a Christian life, but even in the peaceable also, when the servant of God, freed for a while from temptation, in a quiet sweetnesse seeks how to please his God. Thus the parson considering that repentance is the great vertue of the Gospel, and one of the first steps of pleasing God, having for his own use examined the nature of it, is able to explain it after to others. And particularly, having doubted sometimes whether his repentance were true, or at least in that degree it ought to be, since he found himselfe sometimes to weepe more for the losse of some temporall things then for offending God, he came at length to this resolution—that repentance is an act of the mind, not of the body, even as the original signifies; and that the chiefe thing which God in Scriptures requires is the heart and the spirit to worship Him in truth and spirit. Wherefore in case a Christian endeavour to weep, and cannot, since we are not masters of our bodies, this sufficeth. And consequently he found that the essence of repentance, that it may be alike in all God's children (which, as concerning weeping, it cannot be, some being of a more melting temper then others), consisteth in a true detestation of the soul, abhorring and renouncing sin, and turning unto God in truth of heart and newnesse of life; which acts of repentance are and must be found in all God's servants. Not that weeping is not usefull where it can be that so the body may joyn in the grief as it did in the sin; but that so the other acts be, that is not necessary; so that he as truly repents who performs the other acts of repentance, when he cannot more, as he that weeps a floud of tears. This instruction and comfort the parson getting for himself, when he tels it to others becomes a sermon. The like he doth in other Christian vertues, as of faith and love and the cases of conscience belonging thereto, wherein, as St. Paul implyes that he ought (Romans ii.), he first preacheth to himself, and then to others.

CHAP. XXXIV

The Parson's Dexterity in applying of Remedies

THE countrey parson knows that there is a double state of a Christian even in this life, the one military, the other peaceable. The military is when we are assaulted with temptations, either from within or from without. The peaceable is when the divill for a time leaves us, as he did our Saviour, and the angels minister to us their owne food, even joy and peace and comfort in the Holy Ghost. These two states were in our Saviour not only in the beginning of His preaching, but afterwards also; as Matt. xxii. 35, He was tempted, and Luke x. 21, He rejoyced in spirit; and they must be likewise in all that are His. Now the parson having a spirituall judgement, according as he discovers any of his flock to be in one or the other state, so he applies himselfe to them. Those that he findes in the peaceable state he adviseth to be very vigilant, and not to let go the raines as soon as the horse goes easie. Particularly he counselleth them to two things: first, to take heed lest their quiet betray them (as it is apt to do) to a coldnesse and carelessnesse in their devotions, but to labour still to be as fervent in Christian duties as they remember themselves were when affliction did blow the coals; secondly, not to take the full compasse and liberty of their peace; not to eate of all those dishes at table which even their present health otherwise admits, nor to store their house with all those furnitures which even their present plenty of wealth otherwise admits; nor when they are among them that are merry, to extend themselves to all that mirth which the present occasion of wit and company otherwise admits; but to put bounds and hoopes to their joyes; so will they last the longer, and when they depart, returne the sooner. 'If we would judg ourselves, we should not be judged' [1 Cor. xi. 31]; and if we would bound ourselves, we should not be bounded. But if they shall fear that at such or such a time their peace and mirth have carryed them further than this moderation, then to take Job's admirable course, who sacrificed lest his children should have transgressed in their mirth: so let them go and find some poore afflicted soul, and there be bountifull and liberall; for with such sacrifices God is well pleased. Those that the parson finds in the military state he fortifyes and strengthens with his utmost skill. Now in those that are tempted, whatsoever is unruly falls upon two heads: either they think that there is none that can or will look after things, but all goes by chance or wit; or else, though there be a great Governour of all things, yet to them He is lost, as if they said, 'God doth forsake and persecute them, and there is none to deliver them.' If the parson suspect the first, and find sparks of such thoughts now and then to break forth, then, without opposing directly (for disputation is no cure for atheisme), he scatters in his discourse three sorts of arguments, the first taken from nature, the second from the law, the third from grace. For nature, he sees not how a house could be either built without a builder, or kept in repaire without a housekeeper. He conceives not possibly how the windes should blow so much as they can, and the sea rage as much as it can, and all things do what they can, and all, not only without dissolution of the whole, but also of any part, by taking away so much as the usuall seasons of summer and winter, earing and harvest. Let the weather be what it will, still we have bread, though sometimes more, sometimes lesse; wherewith also a carefull Joseph might meet. He conceives not possibly how he that would believe a divinity, if he had been at the creation of all things should lesse beleeve it seeing the preservation of all things; for preservation is a creation; and more, it is a continued creation, and a creation every moment. Secondly, for the law, there may be so evident though unused a proof of Divinity taken from thence, that the atheist or Epicurean can have nothing to contradict. The Jewes yet live, and are known: they have their law and language, bearing witnesse to them, and they to it; they are circumcised to this day, and expect the promises of the Scripture; their countrey also is known, the places and rivers travelled unto and frequented by others, but to them an unpenetrable rock, an unaccessible desert. Wherefore if the Jewes live, all the great wonders of old live in them; and then who can deny the stretched-out arme of a mighty God? especially since it may be a just doubt whether, considering the stubbornnesse of the nation, their living then in their countrey, under so many miracles were a stranger thing then their present exile, and disability to live in their countrey. And it is observable that this very thing was intended by God, that the Jewes should be His proof and witnesses, as He calls them (Isaiah xliii. 12). And their very dispersion in all lands was intended not only for a punishment to them; but for an exciting of others by their sight to the acknowledging of God and His power (Psalm lix. 11); and therefore this kind of punishment was chosen rather then any other. Thirdly, for grace. Besides the continuall succession (since the gospell) of holy men who have born witness to the truth (there being no reason why any should distrust Saint Luke, or Tertullian, or Chrysostome, more then Tully, Virgil, or Livy) there are two prophecies in the Gospel which evidently argue Christ's divinity by their success: the one concerning the woman that spent the oyntment on our Saviour, for which He told that it should never be forgotten, but with the Gospel itselfe be preached to all ages (Matthew xxvi. 13); the other concerning the destruction of Jerusalem, of which our Saviour said, that that generation should not passe till all were fulfilled (Luke xxi. 32); which Josephus his story confirmeth, and the continuance of which verdict is yet evident. To these might be added the preaching of the Gospel in all nations (Matthew xxiv. 14), which we see even miraculously effected in these new discoveryes, God turning men's covetousnesse and ambitions to the effecting of His Word. Now a prophecie is a wonder sent to posterity, leest they complaine of want of wonders. It is a letter sealed and sent, which to the bearer is but paper, but to the receiver and opener is full of power. He that saw Christ open a blind man's eyes saw not more Divinity then he that reads the woman's oyntment in the Gospel or sees Jerusalem destroyed. With some of these heads enlarged and woven into his discourse at severall times and occasions, the parson setleth wavering minds. But if he sees them nearer desperation then atheisme, not so much doubting a God as that He is theirs, then he dives into the boundlesse ocean of God's love, and the unspeakable riches of His loving-kindnesse. He hath one argument unanswerable. If God hate them, either He doth it as they are creatures, dust and ashes, or as they are sinfull. As creatures, He must needs love them; for no perfect artist ever yet hated his owne worke. As sinfull, He must much more love them; because, notwithstanding His infinite hate of sin, His love overcame that hate, and with an exceeding great victory; which in the creation needed not, gave them love for love, even the Son of His love out of His bosome of love. So that man, which way soever he turnes, hath two pledges of God's love, that in the mouth of two or three witnesses every word may be established—the one in his being, the other in his sinfull being; and this as the more faulty in him, so the more glorious in God. And all may certainly conclude that God loves them, till either they despise that love or despaire of His mercy: not any sin else but is within His love; but the despising of love must needs be without it. The thrusting away of His arm makes us onely not embraced.

CHAP. XXXV

The Parson's Condescending

The countrey parson is a lover of old customes, if they be good and harmlesse; and the rather because countrey people are much addicted to them, so that to favour them therein is to win their hearts, and to oppose them therein is to deject them. If there be any ill in the custome that may be severed from the good, he pares the apple, and gives them the clean to feed on. Particularly he loves procession, and maintains it, because there are contained therein 4 manifest advantages: first, a blessing of God for the fruits of the field; secondly, justice in the preservation of bounds; thirdly, charity in loving walking and neighbourly accompanying one another, with reconciling of differences at that time, if there be any; fourthly mercy in releeving the poor by a liberall distribution and largesse, which at that time is or ought to be used. Wherefore he exacts of all to bee present at the perambulation and those that withdraw and sever themselves from it he mislikes, and reproves as uncharitable and unneighbourly; and if they will not reforme, presents them. Nay, he is so farre from condemning such assemblies, that he rather procures them to be often, as knowing that absence breeds strangeness, but presence love. Now love is his business and aime; wherefore he likes well that his parish at good times invite one another to their houses, and he urgeth them to it; and sometimes, where he knowes there hath been or is a little difference, hee takes one of the parties, and goes with him to the other, and all dine or sup together. There is much preaching in this friendliness. Another old custome there is of saying, when light is brought in, 'God send us the light of heaven;' and the parson likes this very well; neither is he affraid of praising or praying to God at all times, but is rather glad of catching opportunities to do them. Light is a great blessing and as great as food, for which we give thanks; and those that thinke this superstitious neither know superstition nor themselves. As for those that are ashamed to use this forme, as being old, and obsolete, and not the fashion, he reformes and teaches them that at baptisme they professed not to be ashamed of Christ's cross, or for any shame to leave that which is good. He that is ashamed in small things will extend his pusillanimity to greater. Rather should a Christian souldier take such occasions to harden himselfe, and to further his exercises of mortification.

CHAP. XXXVI

The Parson Blessing

THE countrey parson wonders that blessing the people is in so little use with his brethren; whereas he thinks it not onely a grave and reverend thing, but a beneficial also. Those who use it not do so either out of niceness, because they like the salutations and complements and formes of worldly language better—which conformity and fashionableness is so exceeding unbefitting a minister, that it deserves reproof, not refutation—or else, because they think it empty and superfluous. But that which the Apostles used so diligently in their writings, nay, which our Saviour Himselfe used (Marke x. 16), cannot bee vain and superfluous. But this was not proper to Christ or the Apostles only, no more then to be a spirituall father was appropriated to them. And if temporall fathers blesse their children, how much more may and ought spirituall fathers! Besides, the priests of the Old Testament were commanded to blesse the people, and the forme thereof is prescribed (Numbers vi. [22–27]). Now as the Apostle argues in another case, if the ministration of condemnation did bless, 'how shall not the ministration of the Spirit exceed in blessing?' [2 Cor. iii. 8]. The fruit of this blessing good Hannah found and received with great joy (1 Samuel i. 18), though it came from a man disallowed by God; for it was not the person, but priesthood, that blessed; so that even ill priests may bless. Neither have the ministers power of blessing only, but also of cursing. So in the Old Testament, Elisha cursed the children (2 Kings ii. 24), which, though our Saviour reproved as unfitting for His particular, Who was to show all humility before His passion, yet He allows it in His Apostles. And therefore St. Peter used that fearful imprecation to Simon Magus (Acts viii. [20–21]), 'Thy mony perish with thee;' and the event confirmed it. So did St. Paul (2 Timothy iv. 14 and 1 Timothy i. 20). Speaking of Alexander the coppersmith, who had withstood his preaching, 'The Lord,' saith he, 'reward him according to his works' [2 Timothy iv. 14]. And again, of Hymeneus and Alexander he saith he had 'delivered them to Satan, that they might learn not to blaspheme.' The formes both of blessing and cursing are expounded in the Common Prayer-book: the one in 'The grace of our Lord Jesus Christ,' &c., and 'The peace of God,' &c.; the other in generall in the Commination. Now blessing differs from prayer in assurance, because it is not performed by way of request, but of confidence and power, effectually applying God's favour to the blessed, by the interesting of that dignity wherewith God hath invested the priest, and ingaging of God's own power and institution for a blessing. The neglect of this duty in ministers themselves hath made the people also neglect it; so that they are so far from craving this benefit from their ghostly father, that they oftentimes goe out of church before he hath blessed them. In the time of Popery, the priest's Benedicite and his holy water were over-highly valued; and now we are fallen to the clean contrary, even from superstition to coldnes and atheism. But the parson first values the gift in himself, and then teacheth his parish to value it. And it is observable that if a minister talke with a great man in the ordinary course of complementing language, he shall be esteemed as ordinary complementers; but if he often interpose a blessing, when the other gives him just opportunity, by speaking any good, this unusuall form begets a reverence, and makes him esteemed according to his profession. The same is to be observed in writing letters also. To conclude, if all men are to blesse upon occasion, as appears, Romans xii. 14, how much more those who are spiritual fathers!

CHAP. XXXVII

Concerning Detraction

The countrey parson perceiving that most, when they are at leasure, make others' faults their entertainment and discourse, and that even some good men think, so they speak truth, they may disclose another's fault, finds it somewhat difficult how to proceed in this point. For if he absolutely shut up men's mouths, and forbid all disclosing of faults, many an evill may not only be, but also spread in his parish, without any remedy (which cannot be applyed without notice), to the dishonor of God and the infection of his flock, and the discomfort, discredit, and hindrance of the pastor. On the other side, if it be unlawful to open faults, no benefit or advantage can make it lawfull; for 'we must not do evill that good may come of it' [Romans iii. 8]. Now the parson taking this point to task, which is so exceeding useful, and hath taken so deep roote that it seems the very life and substance of conversation, hath proceeded thus far in the discussing of it. Faults are either notorious or private. Again, notorious faults are either such as are made known by common fame (and of these, those that know them may talk, so they do it not with sport, but commiseration), or else such as have passed judgment, and been corrected either by whipping or imprisoning or the like. Of these also men may talk, and more—they may discover them to those that know them not; because infamy is a part of the sentence against malefactours, which the Law intends, as is evident by those which are branded for rogues that they may be known, or put into the stocks that they may be looked upon. But some may say, though the Law allow this, the Gospel doth not, which hath so much advanced charity, and ranked backbiters among the generation of the wicked [Romans i. 30]. But this is easily answered: as the executioner is not uncharitable that takes away the life of the condemned, except, besides his office, he add a tincture of private malice, in the joy and haste of acting his part, so neither is he that defames him whom the Law would have defamed, except he also do it out of rancour. For in infamy all are executioners, and the Law gives a malefactour to all to be defamed. And as malefactors may lose and forfeit their goods or life, so may they their good name, and the possession thereof, which before their offence and judgment they had in all men's brests; for all are honest till the contrary be proved. Besides, it concerns the common-wealth that rogues should be known, and charity to the publick hath the precedence of private charity. So that it is so far from being a fault to discover such offenders, that it is a duty rather which may do much good and save much harm. Neverthelesse, if the punished delinquent shall be much troubled for his sins, and turn quite another man, doubtlesse then also men's affections and words must turne, and forbear to speak of that which even God Himself hath forgotten.

THE AUTHOUR'S PRAYER BEFORE SERMON

O Almighty and ever-living Lord God, Majesty and Power and Brightnesse and Glory, how shall we dare to appear before Thy face, who are contrary to Thee in all we call Thee? for we are darknesse, and weaknesse, and filthinesse, and shame. Misery and sin fill our days; yet art Thou our Creatour, and we Thy work. Thy hands both made us, and also made us lords of all Thy creatures; giving us one world in ourselves, and another to serve us: then didst Thou place us in Paradise, and wert proceeding still on in Thy favours, untill we interrupted Thy counsels, disappointed Thy purposes, and sold our God, our glorious, our gracious God, for an apple. O, write it; O, brand it in our foreheads for ever: for an apple once we lost our God, and still lose Him for no more—for money, for meat, for diet. But Thou, Lord, art patience and pity and sweetnesse and love; therefore we sons of men are not consumed. Thou hast exalted Thy mercy above all things, and hast made our salvation, not our punishment, Thy glory; so that then where sin abounded, not death, but grace superabounded: accordingly when we had sinned beyond any help in heaven or earth, then Thou saidst, 'Lo, I come!' then did the Lord of life, unable of Himselfe to die, contrive to do it. He took flesh, He wept, He died; for His enemies He died; even for those that derided Him then, and still despise Him. Blessed Saviour! many waters could not quench Thy love, nor no pit overwhelme it. But though the streams of Thy blood were current through darknesse, grave, and hell, yet by these Thy conflicts and seemingly hazards didst Thou arise triumphant and therein mad'st us victorious.

Neither doth Thy love yet stay here; for this word of Thy rich peace and reconciliation Thou hast committed, not to thunder or angels, but to silly and sinful men, even to me, pardoning my sins, and bidding me go feed the people of Thy love.

Blessed be the God of heaven and earth, Who onely doth wondrous things. Awake, therefore, my lute and my viol; awake, all my powers, to glorify Thee. We praise Thee, we bless Thee, we magnifie Thee for ever; and now, O Lord, in the power of Thy victories, and in the wayes of Thy ordinances, and in the truth of Thy love, lo, we stand here, beseeching Thee to blesse Thy word wherever spoken this day throughout the universall Church. O, make it a word of power and peace, to convert those who art not yet Thine, and to confirme those that are; particularly blesse it in this Thy own kingdom, which Thou hast made a Land of light, a storehouse of Thy treasures and mercies. O, let not our foolish and unworthy hearts rob us of the continuance of this Thy sweet love; but pardon our sins, and perfect what Thou hast begun. Ride on, Lord, because of the word of truth, and meeknesse, and righteousnesse, 'and Thy right hand shall teach Thee terrible things' [Psalm xlv. 4]. Especially blesse this portion here assembled together, with Thy unworthy servant speaking unto them. Lord Jesu, teach Thou me, that I may teach them; sanctifie and enable all my powers, that in their full strength they may deliver Thy message reverently, readily, faithfully, and fruitfully. O, make Thy word a swift word, passing from the ear to the heart, from the heart to the life and conversation; that as the rain returns not empty, so neither may Thy word, but accomplish that for which it is given. O Lord, hear; O Lord, forgive; O Lord, hearken; and do so for Thy blessed Son's sake, in Whose sweet and pleasing words we say, 'Our Father,' &c.

PRAYER AFTER SERMON

BLESSED be God and the Father of all mercy, Who continueth to pour His benefits upon us. Thou hast elected us, Thou hast called us, Thou hast justified us, sanctified and glorified us; Thou wast born for us, and Thou livedst and diedst for us; Thou hast given us the blessings of this life and of a better. O Lord, Thy blessings hang in clusters, they come trooping upon us, they break forth like mighty waters on every side. And now, Lord, Thou hast fed us with the bread of life; so man did eat angels' food. O Lord, bless it; O Lord, make it health and strength unto us; still striving and prospering so long within us, untill our obedience reach Thy measure of Thy love, Who hast done for us as much as may be. Grant this, dear Father, for Thy Son's sake, our only Saviour, to Whom with Thee and the Holy Ghost, three Persons but one most glorious incomprehensible God, be ascribed all honour, and glory, and praise, ever. Amen.

NOTE

It is recorded in Izaak Walton's 'Life of Mr. George Herbert' that 'Mr. Farrer' . . . [Nicholas Ferrar of Little Gidding] 'hearing of Mr. Herbert's sickness, sent Mr. Edmund Duncon . . . from his house of Gidden Hall, which is near to Huntingdon, to see Mr. Herbert, and to assure him he wanted not his daily prayers for his recovery; and Mr. Duncon was to return back to Gidden with an account of Mr. Herbert's condition.' After a few days at Bath Mr. Duncon called again on his way back, and Mr. Herbert then 'did, with so sweet a humility as seemed to exalt him, bow down to Mr. Duncon, and with a thoughtful and contented look, say to him, "Sir, I pray deliver this little book to my dear brother Farrer, and tell him, he shall find in it a picture of the many spiritual conflicts that have passed betwixt God and my soul, before I could subject mine to the will of Jesus my Master: in whose service I have now found perfect freedom. Desire him to read it; and then, if he can think it may turn to the advantage of any dejected poor soul, let it be made public; if not, let him burn it, for I and it are less than the least of God's mercies." Thus meanly did this humble man think of this excellent book, which now bears the name of "The Temple."'

This visit occurred about three weeks before George Herbert's death, and consequently he did not live to see his 'little book' in print. The MS. given to Edmund Duncon does not seem to be in existence, and the material for the text is as follows:—

(*a*) The Bodleian MS., a copy prepared, probably, for presentation to the Vice-Chancellor, for the purpose of obtaining his licence.

(*b*) A little Gidding-bound volume now in the Dr. Williams Library, London, containing about half the poems which constitute 'The Temple,' and other poems, with corrections in Herbert's handwriting.

(*c*) The book published by Nicholas Ferrar. It is assumed that Ferrar caused a few copies to be struck off for private friends before issuing the book to the public, since a copy is in existence with an undated title-page, on which the author is described as 'late Oratour of the Universitie of *Cambridge*.' Its imprint is as follows:—'CAMBRIDGE: | Printed by *Thomas Buck* | and *Roger Daniel*: | ¶And are to be ſold by *Francis* | *Green*, ſtationer in | *Cambridge*.' Of this undated copy the Rev. A. B. Grosart issued a facsimile reprint. It does not differ, save in the imprints and the author's description, from that issued to the public dated 1633, which is practically the first edition, and the one here reprinted. In eight years from the date of the first issue six editions had been published and, writing in 1670, when, as a rule, publishers did not dispose of *x* editions before the day of publication, Walton says 'there have been more than twenty thousand of them sold since the first impression.'

'When Mr. Farrer sent this book to Cambridge to

be licensed for the press, the Vice-Chancellor would by no means allow the two so much noted verses,

> "Religion stands a tiptoe in our land,
> Ready to pass to the American strand,"

to be printed; and Mr. Farrer would by no means allow the book to be printed and want them. But after some time, and some arguments for and against their being made public, the Vice-Chancellor said, "I knew Mr. Herbert well, and know that he had many heavenly speculations, and was a divine poet: but I hope the world will not take him to be an inspired prophet, and therefore I license the whole book."'

In a book so full of personal utterance it seems needless to single out any poem for specific mention, but 'Affliction' (p. 40), 'The Pearl,' 'The Priesthood,' 'The Crosse,' and 'The Glance,' may be named as of autobiographic value, and 'Aaron' as typical of Herbert's individual genius and thought.

No edition of 'The Temple' is complete without its prose counterpart, 'A Priest to the Temple,' and it has therefore been included in the present issue. It is 'a book so full of plain, prudent, and useful rules, that that Country Parson, that can spare twelve pence, and yet wants it, is scarce excusable' (Walton).

The text here reprinted of 'A Priest to the Temple' is based upon Dr. Alexander B. Grosart's, itself a reproduction of the first edition (1652). The original issue is a duodecimo 'Printed by *T. Maxey* for *T. Garthwait*, at the little North door of St. *Paul's*.'

'A prefatory view of the life and vertues of the authour, and excellencies of this book' (unsigned) by Barnabas Oley, Vicar of Great Gransden, was prefixed to the first edition. 'A preface to the Christian reader, consisting of six paragraphs,' by the same writer and signed, was added to the second edition, 1671, and (enlarged) to the third edition, 1675.

Following this note will be found a brief summary of the events of George Herbert's life, with a few illustrative quotations from Walton's 'Life' of him: a few notse on the text complete the edition. The reader may be referred to an edition of 'The Temple' by Dr. Gibson, Vicar of Leeds (Methuen & Co.), for alternative readings from the Bodleian and Williams MSS., to the edition with notes by Coleridge, published by Pickering in 1835, to Coleridge's 'The Friend' and his 'Biographia Literaria,' and to the editions supervised by the Rev. A. B. Grosart in the 'Fuller Worthies Library' (1874), and in Bell's Aldine Series; Prof. Mayor's 'Nicholas Ferrar: Two Lives by his brother John and by Dr. Jebb' (Camb. 1855), may also be consulted with interest.

It is said that Charles the First when in captivity 'read often in Herbert's Divine poems,' and, though Herbert was not fortunate enough to meet with the approval of Addison and of Dr. Johnson, he influenced writers so wide apart as Keble and Baxter, he inspired Vaughan and Crashaw, and he has been a solace to many.

A. R. W.

INDEX OF WORDS

PAGE

vii. *The Printers to the Reader.* This preface was written by Nicholas Ferrar.

1. *Perirrhanterium*, an instrument for sprinkling holy water.

2. *keep the round*, pass the bottle round.
lose, loose.

4. *thy native cloth.* English cloth has always been held in esteem.
gone to grasse, turned out to grass like a horse.
ship them over, send them abroad.

5. *stowre*, inflexible, stubborn.
shelf, reef, *i.e.* rock on which he is wrecked.
the clue undoes, the ball unrolls.
sconses, bulwarks, outworks.

6. *under-writes*, subscribes to.
sickly healths, injurious, health-drinking.

7. *Take starres for money*, the treasure which is in heaven.
makes his cloth too wide, is extravagant in his dress.
bear the bell, carry the prize.
curiousnesse, affectation.
herauld, the government commissioner who went round to inquire into matters of arms.

8, etc., *complexion*, disposition.
allay, alloy.
pos'd, brought to a standstill.
webbe . . . poysonous. Spiders' webs were formerly thought venomous.
the great souldier's honour. Dr. Grosart suggests that Themistocles is meant 'before Salamis, and his memorable "Strike, but hear me."'

9. *The fine*, that which is left when the 'scumme' is taken away.
etc., *sad*, severe, solid.
parcell-devil, one who goes shares with the devil.

INDEX OF WORDS

PAGE

11. *lose his rest*, lose his wager (in the card game of primero).

11, 263. *wittie*, wise.

12. *Pitch thy behaviour low*. *Cf.* 'A Priest to the Temple': *The Authour to the Reader.*

means, aims at.

13. *market-money*, market price, lowest price.

14. *six and seven*, sixes and sevens, worldly affairs.

15, 87. *seal*, in falconry, to sew up a hawk's eyes.

17. *Superliminare*, the doorway lintel. *Cf.* Exodus xii. 22.

Avoid, avaunt.

21. *my enmitie*, enmity towards Me.

25. *weeds*, clothing.

28. *preventest*, anticipates.

29. *spittle*, hospital.

mend common wayes. The provision of money for road-mending was a charitable act.

My musick shall finde thee. 'The Sunday before his death he rose suddenly from his bed or couch, called for one of his instruments, took it into his hand and said,

"My God, my God,
My music shall find thee,
And every string
Shall have his attribute to sing."

And having tuned it, he played and sung:

"The Sundays of man's life,
Threaded together on time's string,
Make bracelets to adorn the wife
Of the eternal glorious King:
On Sundays Heaven's doors stand ope;
Blessings are plentiful and rife,
More plentiful than hope."

Thus he sung on earth such Hymns and Anthems as the Angels, and he, and Mr. Farrer, now sing in Heaven' (Walton).

31. *set . . . abroach*, set running.

37. *imp my wing*. In falconry to imp=to add feathers to a hawk's wing.

38. *Behither ill*, except ill, well on this side of evil.

INDEX OF WORDS

PAGE

38. *made a partie*, caused a faction.
    began unto, challenged.
42. *crosse-bias*, divert, turn aside.
44. *a rare outlandish root*, 'the snake-root of Virginia . . . "a most certain and present remedy against the venome of the rattle-snake" (Parkinson : "Theatr. Botan.").'—Grosart.
49. *disseized*, deprived.
51. *race*, raze.
52. *pull for Prime*, drew cards, in the old game of primero.
54. *Lidger*, ambassador.
    handsell, an earnest-penny.
    watch a potion. A corrupt line; no intelligible meaning can be found, nor has a reasonable substitute for 'watch' or 'potion' been suggested.
55. *braves*, effrontery.
57. *broken pay*, instalments.
58. *imprest*, earnest-money, as that given to a soldier 'pressed' into service.
61. *Ieat*, jet.
64. *anneal in glasse*, fix colours in glass by heat.
65. *a cloisters gates*, a reference to the Emperor Charles V.
66. *Quidditie*, trifle, nice refinement.
67. *Mansuetude*, gentleness.
    bandying, combining.
    amerc'd, fined.
68. *weeds*, clothing.
    Who is the honest man? Herbert's stepfather, Sir John Danvers.
69. *tentations*, temptations.
    bias, divergent.
70. *tallies*, notched sticks by which accounts were kept.
    The sigh, a reference to the old idea that sighing decreased strength.
72. *thy release*, the release granted by Sunday.
73. *The Sundaies of mans life.* *Cf.* Note to p. 29.
77. *That busie plant.* Because flowers and fruit are borne at the same time.
80. *For by that powder.* Dr. Grosart suggests this 'may refer to the blowing of powders, sugar of lead, sugars, etc., into the eyes of horses and dogs, when their eyes are dimmed by a film or partial opacity.'

INDEX OF WORDS

PAGE

82. *Sommers.* The main planks or girders in a floor, which hold the joists.
shor'd, supported.
83. *aspects.* The appearances of the planets in their relation to each other, and therefore in their supposed influence on earthly matters.
85. *Vertue.* Lovers of Walton will remember how he introduces this poem in 'The Compleat Angler.'
87. *silk-twist.* *Cf.* Ariadne's silken guide through the Labyrinth.
89. *to whose creation*, by whose deeds.
no fruit. In the Williams MS. these words are 'more fruit.' It is probable, therefore, that 'no' was read for 'mo'=more.
90. *kinde*, kin.
92. *pretendeth to*, seeks after.
94. *disseize*, deprive.
95. *take one from ten.* An allusion to the tithe or tenth part contributed to church uses.
96. *store*, stakes.
98. *Marking*, noticing, looking towards.
101. *posie*, motto.
shelf, reef.
102. *burnish*, spread abroad, flourish.
105. *bill*, billhook.
110. *Quip*, sharp pleasantry.
115. *waving*, wavering,
savour, knowledge.
117. *annealed*, burnt or fired in.
119. *prevent*, forestall, come before.
bouls, bowls.
121. *good cheap*, very cheap, *bon marché*.
, and 138. *broach*, tap, let forth.
122. *marry*, are the connecting link between.
mines, th' earth and plants. As Dr. Grosart points out, an allusion to the old idea that ores grow.
Crocodile . . . Elephant. Popular ideas current in Herbert's time, which have no basis in fact.
owes, owns.
123. *optick*, magnifying glass.
cockatrice, a fabulous monster, hatched from a cock's egg under a serpent.

INDEX OF WORDS

PAGE

125. *wants*, lacks.

129. *snudge*, lie snug, mind his own business.

130. *like a Dolphins skinne.* The *Coryphene* (a relation of the mackerel) show beautiful metallic colours whether in the water or when justifying the phrase, 'the dying dolphin's changing hues.' The Cetacean 'dolphin' is an entirely different creature.

135. *object their crimes*, place their crimes before them.

140. *noise . . . part.* The words are used as of a band of musicians.

pulling, puling.

142. *fraught*, freight.

143. *If comforts fell.* The line which should follow this is missing. Dr. Grosart suggests, 'Did at all times fall.'

144. *articling*, making of articles of treaty.

146. *Dishes . . . beam . . . scape.* The scape is the upright part of the scales; the 'dishes' hang from the beam.

The Pilgrimage. A forerunner of Bunyan's 'Pilgrim's Progress.'

147. *Angell*, a gold coin, bearing the image of an angel, worth about ten shillings. Perhaps also used in a double sense.

149. *licorous*, desiring.

153. *All-heal.* The mistletoe was so called by the Druids on account of its medicinal qualities.

157. *light*, alight.

158. *cyens*, scions.

159. *Of what is fit.* The punctuation should be after 'not,' not after 'fit.'

165. *at use*, at usury.

170. *ring*, fence, that which surrounds.

charge, burden.

173. *their own demean*, the qualities they themselves possess and show forth.

174. *Chases in Arras*, hunting scenes on tapestry.

career, race.

177. *means*, aims at.

179. *prevent*, forestall.

182. *dash*, bedaub.

Light and perfections. *Cf.* Exodus xxviii. 30.

noise. See note to p. 140.

INDEX OF WORDS

PAGE

183. *Amber-greese.* A substance found on sea-shores or floating on the seas, and highly valued as a perfume. It is probably a secretion of the spermaceti whale.

184, 191. *Pomander*, a scent-box or ball.

185. *The harbingers are come.* The barbinger was 'an officer of the king's household who went before to allot and "mark" the lodgings of the king's attendants in a "Progress."'—Grosart.

185, 204. *Dispark*, dispossess.
I passe not, I care not.

186. *canvas . . . arras.* In hangings, canvas was painted cloth, arras woven tapestry.

192. *my posie.* *Cf.* George Herbert's words when he handed the MS. of 'The Temple' to Edmund Duncon (p. 295).
A Parodie. The poem 'parodied' is one of Donne's.

194. *prepossest*, owner of it previously.

196. *Tarantulaes*, venomous spiders whose bite was believed to be cured by music.

197. *peculiar*, own.

201. *Christ-Crosse*=criss-cross, a horn-book alphabet.

204. *a rogue*, Mahomet.

205. *a prophet.* A reference to the Greek Oracles.

207. *Jurie*, Jewry.
Religion stands on tip-toe in our land. These lines well-nigh prevented 'The Temple' from being licensed by the Cambridge Vice-Chancellor. (See p. 297).

208. *sound*, sea-inlet, used in the sense of a haven.

214. *hee shoots higher.* *Cf.* 'The Church-Porch,' p. 12.

217. *revoking*, calling back.

220. *travell*, travail, labour.

224. *treatable*, prolonged.
etc. *presented*, informed against, for the purpose of action being taken.

225. *slubbering*, slovenly.
pausably, with due pause.

230. *induce it*, bring it in.

233. *experiment*, experience.

234. *happily*, haply.

235. *Chamber of London.* The Treasury of the City of London, in George Herbert's day a synonym of security, equivalent to the present use of the term 'Bank of England.'

INDEX OF WORDS

PAGE

236. *boards a child*, is treated almost like a child.
249. *censure*, judgment.
suppling, soothing.
250. *set*, rated.
very respectively, with great respect.
251. *brief*, Letters patent, authorising charitable collections.
252. *tester*, sixpence.
254. *silly*, ignorant, uneducated.
in vertue, in essence.
256. *course*, coarse.
257. *puts up to an Apostle*, apes being an Apostle.
258. *Dalton's 'Justice of Peace.'* Michael Dalton's (1554-1620) 'Country Justice' was published in 1618.
259. *one anatomy*, a dissected corpse.
Fernelius (1497–1558), a celebrated French physician.
260. *bolearmena*, an astringent Armenian earth.
261. *reduce*, lead back.
262. *consters*, construes.
264. *baned*, diseased or poisonous.
266. *Gerson* (1363–1429), a French theological writer, one of the reputed authors of 'The Imitation of Christ,' author of 'The Consolation of Theology.'
267. *defixed*, firmly fixed.
soyle, manure.
271. *reduce*, lead, induce.
272. *imbarn*, *inned*, barned.
273. *the exigent*, his [the man's] exigency.
276. *drowning*, irrigating, flooding.
277. *graffe*, graft.
279. *those new Plantations*, Virginia.
282. *hoopes*, confines.
283. *earing*, ploughing. *Cf.* Gen. xlv. 6.
286. *procession*, beating the bounds.
292. *silly*, ignorant.

A LIST OF DATES

1593 April 3rd. George Herbert born in Montgomery Castle, Wales. His eldest brother was Lord Herbert of Cherbury. Of his mother Donne wrote—

'No Spring nor Summer-beauty hath such grace
As I have seen in an Autumnal face.'

1594 *Hooker's 'Ecclesiastical Polity.'*

1597 Sir Richard Herbert, George Herbert's father, died.

1597 *Bacon's 'Essays.'*

1609 After a time of preparation at home and at Westminster, he was admitted scholar, May 5th, and matriculated pensioner at Trinity College, Cambridge, December 18th.

1611 *Authorised Version of the Bible.*

1612–13 Bachelor of Arts

1615 Elected Fellow of his college.

1616 Master of Arts.

1616 *Death of Shakespeare.*

1620 January 18th, appointed Public Orator. He kept this office until 1627.

1620 *The Pilgrim Fathers land in New England.* See p. 207.
Bacon's 'Novum Organum.'

'In this time of Mr. Herbert's attendance and expectation of some good occasion to remove from Cambridge to Court, God, in whom there is an unseen chain of causes, did in a short time put an end to the lives of two of his most obliging and most powerful friends, Lodowick Duke of Richmond, and James Marquis of Hamilton; and not long after him King James died also [1625], and with them, all Mr. Herbert's Court hopes.'

1626 July 15 'Made [lay] Prebend of Layton Ecclesia, in the Diocese of Lincoln.'

A LIST OF DATES

1627 June. His mother died. Her Funeral Sermon was preached by Donne. Herbert's Greek and Latin poems to her memory were published with the sermon.

C. 1614 *Sir Henry Wotton's 'Character of a Happy Life.'*

C. 1629 'About the year 1629, and the thirty-fourth of his age, Mr. Herbert was seized with a sharp quotidian ague.' To cure this he went to Woodford, Essex, where he remained for a year.

1629 *Milton's Ode 'On the Morning of Christ's Nativity.'*

1629 Went to Dauntsey, Wilts, to Lord Danvers, Earl of Danby, 'who loved Mr. Herbert . . very much.' Here his health improved, and on March 5th, three days after he saw her, he married, at Edlington, Jane Danvers, a daughter of Charles Danvers, of Bainton, Wilts, a kinsman of the Earl of Danby.

She inspired 'an unfeigned love, and a serviceable respect from all that conversed with her; and this love followed her in all places, as inseparably as shadows follow substances in sunshine.'

1630 April 26th. After taking holy orders he was, through the influence of his kinsman, the Earl of Pembroke, 'inducted into the good, and more pleasant than healthful, parsonage of Bemerton; which is a mile from Salisbury.' The church is dedicated to St. Andrew.

'When at his induction he was shut into Bemerton Church, being left there alone to toll the bell,—as the Law requires him,—he staid so much longer than an ordinary time, before he returned to those friends that staid expecting him at the Church-door, that his friend Mr. Woodnot looked in at the Church-window, and saw him lie prostrate on the ground before the Altar; at which time and place . . . he set some rules to himself, for the future manage of his life.'

He now 'changed his sword and silk clothes into a canonical coat,' and lived that life of 'a country parson' of which Walton has given so delightful an account.

1633 'Mr. George Herbert, Esq., Parson of Fuggleston and Bemerton, was buried 3d day of March.' (Parish Register.)

'He lyes in the chancell, under no large nor yet very good marble grave-stone, without any inscription. . . . He was buryed, according to his owne desire, with the singing service for the buriall of the dead by the singing men of Sarum.' (Aubrey Letters, ii. 80–1.)

'I wish—if God shall be so pleased—that I may be so happy as to die like him. Iz. Wa.'

Herbert 'was for his person of a stature inclining towards tallness; his body was very straight, and so far from being cumbered with too much flesh, that he was lean to an extremity. His aspect was cheerful, and his speech and motion did both declare him a gentleman; for they were all so meek and obliging, that they purchased love and respect from all that knew him.'

During his last illness the following prayer was offered up for him daily in the Little Gidding household (Nicholas Ferrar's):—

'O most mighty God and merciful Father, we most humbly beseech Thee, if it be Thy good pleasure, to continue to us that singular benefit which Thou hast given us in the friendship of Thy servant, our deer brother, who now lieth on the bed of sickness. Let him abide with us yet awhile, for the furtherance of our faith. We have indeed deserved by our ingratitude not only the loss of him, but whatever other opportunities Thou hast given us for the attainment of our salvation. We do not deserve to be heard in our supplications; but Thy mercies are above all Thy works. In consideration whereof we prostrate ourselves in all humble earnestness, beseeching Thee, if so it may seem good to Thy Divine Majesty, that Thou wilt hear us in this, Who hast heard us in all the rest, and that Thou wilt bring him back again from the gates of death; that Thou wilt yet awhile spare him, that he may live to Thy honour and our comfort. Lord, Thou hast willed that our delights should be in the saints on earth and in such as excel in virtue; how, then, should we not be afflicted and mourn when Thou takest them away from us? Thou hast made him a great help and furtherance of the best things amongst us: how, then, can we but esteem the loss of him a chastisement from Thy displeasure? O Lord, we beseech Thee it may not be so: We beseech Thee, if it be Thy good pleasure, restore unto us our dear brother, by restoring to him his health; so will we praise and magnify Thy name and mercy with a song of thanksgiving. Hear us, O Lord, for Thy dear Son's sake, Jesus Christ our Saviour. Amen.'

1636 Herbert's Translation of Lud. Cornarus's 'Treatise of Temperance and Sobrietie' published.

1638 Herbert's Letter to Nicholas Ferrar and 'Briefe Notes' on Valdesso's 'Hundred and ten Considerations Treating of Those things which are most profitable, most necessary, and most perfect in our Christian Profession' published.

1640 'Outlandish Proverbs, selected by Mr. G. H.' published. A second edition, entitled 'Jacula Prudentum or Outlandish Proverbs, Sentences, etc., Selected by Mr. George Herbert,' was published in 1651. These and the minor works abovementioned, together with sundry 'Orations' and Letters, will be found in the Rev. A. B. Grosart's edition of Herbert, in the "Fuller Worthies Library" edition.

1670 Izaak Walton's 'Life of Mr. George Herbert.'

CPSIA information can be obtained
at www.ICGtesting.com
Printed in the USA
BVHW040506250520
580235BV00003B/36